Königs Erläuterungen und Materialien
Band 482

Erläuterungen zu

Paul Auster
Moon Palace

von Maria-Felicitas Herforth

Bange Verlag

Über die Autorin dieser Erläuterung:

Maria-Felicitas Herforth, geboren 1980, Studium der Anglistik und Germanistik an der Ruhr-Universität Bochum (1999–2005), Studienaufenthalt in Großbritannien (2001–2002), 2005–2006 Doktorandin und wissenschaftliche Hilfskraft im Englischen Seminar der Ruhr-Universität Bochum, 2007–2009 Referendarin in den Fächern Englisch und Deutsch, seit 2009 Studienrätin in Bochum, Autorin von Königs Erläuterungen.

1. Auflage 2009
ISBN: 978-3-8044-1887-5

Titelabbildung: Paul Auster
Druck und Weiterverarbeitung: Tiskárna Akcent, Vimperk

Preface

Paul Auster's novel *Moon Palace* was published in 1989. Marco Stanley Fogg's discovery of his heritage in a reality which is dominated by chance and experienced in fragments is the American author's most renowned work, along with his famous detective stories from the *New York Trilogy*. The reader is drawn into a diverse complex narrative consisting of reflections, biographies and allusions to historical and cultural-historical events and characters, with scenes from Wild West mythology and life in the metropolis of the East.
The purpose of this book is to facilitate an understanding of this work of contemporary American literature. It discusses the most important topics and structural principles and can be used either for additional background knowledge or as material in class. Given its rich diversity, particular emphasis has been placed hereby on the text analysis of *Moon Palace*. Complicated contexts are drawn together and are clarified in chart form (see chapter 1.3 and 2.3). The analysis is based on Faber and Faber's edition of *Moon Palace* (Faber and Faber Limited, London, 1990). Annotations can be found in chapter 2.5 and page numbers are cited to facilitate the understanding of the novel. Secondary literature is quoted in the footnotes. Finally, chapter 3 should enable the reader to put his/her comprehension of *Moon Palace* to the test.

1. Paul Auster: Life and works

1.1 Biography

Year	Place	Event	Age
1947	Newark, New Jersey	The writer and director Paul Benjamin Auster is born in Newark/ New Jersey on 3rd February, the son of a middle class American family. His ancestors are Austrian Jews who immigrated to the USA around 1890. After his parents split in the mid-1960s, Paul and his sister live with their mother.	
1966	Travels through Europe	Following his graduation from High School in Newark Paul Auster travels to Europe (Paris, Spain, Dublin).	19
1966-1970	New York	Auster studies English and Literature at Columbia University/ New York.	19-23
1970		After graduating with an MA, he works as a sailor on an oil tanker.	23

Year	Place	Event	Age
1971-1974	Paris	Auster lives in France with his wife-to-be, Lydia Davis. He earns a living translating French lyrics as well as writing his own poetry.	24-27
1974-1980	New York	In 1974 Paul Auster returns to the USA with Lydia Davis. They marry on 6th October 1974 and have a son, Daniel. Auster is given a teaching position at Columbia University and works as a translator and writer of French literature *(Blanchot, Dupin, Mallarmé, Sartre amongst others)*. During this time, Auster writes foremost lyric poetry; *Unearth* (1974), *Wall Writing* (1976), *Facing the Music* (1980).	27-33
1981		After the end of his marriage to Lydia Davis, Auster meets the writer Siri Hustvedt (born in 1955, Minnesota) whom he marries in 1983. They have a daughter, Sophie.	34

Year	Place	Event	Age
1982		The autobiographical collections of essays are published: *The Inventions of Solitude* (1982) and *The Art of Hunger: Essays, Prefaces, Interviews* (1982).	35
1986-1990	New Jersey	Paul Auster starts a teaching position at Princeton University/New Jersey. Additional work as a successful film-maker. During this time he writes the following novels: *The New York Trilogy* (1987), *In the Country of Last Things* (1987), *Moon Palace* (1989) and *The Music of Chance* (1990).	39-43
1995-1998	Brooklyn/New York	Auster's screenplays *Smoke/Blue in the Face* (1995) and *Lulu on the Bridge* (1998) are released.	48-51
2005		The novel *The Brooklyn Follies* is published.	58
2006		Today, Paul Auster lives with his family in Brooklyn/New York.[1]	59

1 Cf. Paul Auster's homepage http://www.paulauster.co.uk/ [August 2006] and http://de.wikipedia.org/wiki/Paul_Auster. [August 2006]

1.2 Historical background

The following summary gives an overview of the most important historical events against which the novel is set. This is intended to complement the reader's background knowledge, as well as to explain any unclear circumstances that may result from the subjective narrative of the first-person narrator[2].

The Vietnam War (1964-1975)
The Vietnam War is generally understood to be the deployment of the US military against the
so-called Vietcong and the armed forces of North Vietnam between 1964 and 1975. However, the American mission in Vietnam really started in 1955 when a few US military advisors came to South Vietnam to support the government, which was under pressure from the Communist North of the country. North Vietnam was being supported at the time by the USSR and China. After Mao Tse-tung's victory in China, the US government, fearful that it might lose Vietnam to Communism (Domino effect theory), began supporting the South militarily as well as economically. The Communist resistance in South Vietnam responded by founding the *Front National de Liberation du Viet-nam Sud* (NLF, National Liberation Front of South Vietnam), the military wing of which was named Viêt Nam Công San (Vietnamese Communists) or Vietcong. The Vietcong was at war with the government of South Vietnam and their army. Aware of the government's weak position and their lack of support from the predominantly rural population, the US government immediately increased their military aid.

2 For further study cf. e.g. Wasser, Hartmut (Hg.): *USA: Grundwissen – Länderkunde – Wirtschaft – Gesellschaft*. Opladen: Leske + Budrich, 2000, Coleman, William S.E., *Voices of Wounded Knee* (Lincoln: University of Nebraska Press, 2000), http://www.oberschulamt-freiburg.de/gym/faecher/english/engl_jae/auster/_start.htm [August 2006]

In 1964 the Vietnam War escalated, and the US Congress took the decision to allow President Lyndon B. Johnson to make his own decisions. So in 1965, the US Air force joined the Vietnam War by bombing the Hô-Chí-Min-Path (*Operation Rolling Thunder*) and US combat troops (by 1967, up to 500.000) started arriving. The US army's attempts to defeat the North Vietnamese army by intensive air strikes and *Agent Orange* (a herbicide for the defoliation of trees) were unsuccessful. The actions of the US army hit the civilian population harder than it did the Vietcong. The massacre of civilians in the village of My Lai at the hands of American soldiers and the coverage in the press led to worldwide protests against the US involvement in Vietnam.
Domestic pressure led to the war being 'de-Americanized: The US administration decided to withdraw its troops bit by bit and to hand power back to the South Vietnamese army. Nevertheless, American intervention lasted until 1973. In 1975, the civil war ended with the victory of the Communist North. The Americans had lost over 58.000 soldiers in combat, the Vietnamese loss was estimated to be between 1,5 and 5 million soldiers and civilians. Even today, the Vietnam War is still seen as a prime example of a war by proxy in the Cold War between East and West. In the novel *Moon Palace*, Fogg temporarily fears his conscription and with it "an early death in the jungles of Asia" (p. 20). The war in Vietnam is also one of the reasons for the protest movement of the 1960s in which Fogg takes part *(see p.38)*.

Student protests and protest movements in the 1960s (USA)
America's open approach policy to their mission in Vietnam, with war reporters accompanying the fighting troops, brought the real atrocities of war home to the American public. The US military's use of Napalm (firebombs), which primarily harmed the civilians, and war crimes, such as that of My Lai, caused

public outrage and led to protests worldwide, as well as in the US. The US government was accused of leading a war against the civilians rather than against the Communist enemy.
The anti-(Vietnam-)war protests were part of a general protest movement that began in the late 1960s when students started rebelling against the 'elite' and demanded a change to what they saw as authoritarian social structures. This revolution coincided with the Afro-American movement and led to monumental protests. They primarily focused on

- the Vietnam War,
- the Cold War and the nuclear arms race between the USA and the USSR,
- defying outdated conventions, norms and values as well as fighting against social injustice,
- the economy and the power of the mass media, and their impact on society,
- consumption and environmental pollution.

The protest movement culminated between 1966 and 1969. From 1968 onwards, the majority of the American population advocated a withdrawal of American troops from Vietnam.

Moon Landing (20th July 1969)
With their 'Apollo Space programme', the USA were hoping to beat the USSR in the race to the moon. The aim of this programme was to land a man on the moon. The Soviet Union were pursuing the same goal and had been in the lead since the launch of the Sputnik in 1957. Shortly after the first manned spaceflight by Juri Gagarin in April 1961, President Kennedy announced that a moon landing would take place before the end of the century, thus launching the Apollo project. On 20th July 1969, Neil Armstrong and Edwin Aldrin were the first men to

land on the moon. As the Soviet Union had been unable to set up their own space programme, America won the 'space race'. The moon landing was generally seen as America's demonstration of strength and ability in the field of science and technology. In *Moon Palace*, Fogg experiences the moon landing ambivalently (see section 2.3.5 of this book).

The history of the USA's colonialisation

After Christopher Columbus (re-)discovered America in 1492, people from everywhere, but especially from Europe, began immigrating to the New World. During President Thomas Jefferson's term in office (1801-1809) the new nation focused on 'the winning of the West'. The intention was to populate the American West. The settlement of the land was implemented in three stages:

- trappers, hunters and missionaries completed the pioneering work,
- squatters occupied undeveloped government land and cultivated it,
- squatters sold the land on in order to move further west.

Step by step, the whole of the American West was populated by European settlers. To this day, the colonialisation of the West has a symbolic significance for American society and is legendary. Democracy is equated with the so-called "frontier experiences", which are seen as the birthplace of the social equality and autonomy that resulted from the settlement of the land. This is what is generally known as the 'pioneering spirit'.

However, there was also a huge downside to the colonialisation of the West. The European colonial powers waged a war against the Native Americans, wherever their expansionist plans were met with opposition. By using superior 'arms' (guns vs. bow and

arrow) as well as infectious diseases, the Native Americans were pushed off their land in often bloody conflicts.
By the end of the 19th century, the settlers had subordinated the Native Americans. During the course of the history of American colonialisation, they were either wiped out or placed on reservations which were often inhospitable. On 29th December 1890, over 290 Native Americans, men, women and children, were killed by the US army at Wounded Knee on the Pine-Ridge reservation in South Dakota. This battle marked the end of the war. For more information on the East-to-West movement, the 'frontier experience' as well as the American Natives (see also chapter 2.3.5).

1.3 *Moon Palace* and other works by Paul Auster

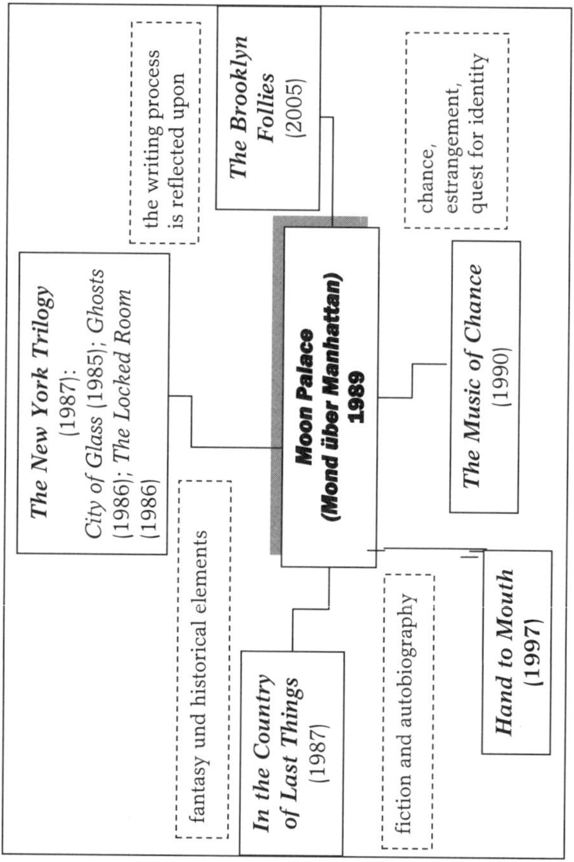

2. Text analysis and interpretation

2.1 Genesis and Sources

Paul Auster spent about 20 years working on *Moon Palace*, from the early 1970s to the late 1980s. During this time he also wrote *Last Legs, Luna, Columbus's Egg*, as well as several versions of *Moon Palace*[3]. The first drafts stem from Auster's student days and contain material that can be found in *City of Glass* (1985) and in *In the Country of Last Things* (1987):

> *"The original* Moon Palace *was enormous; it would've been three times the length it is now. There were lots of bits in it that I stole and used in* City of Glass. *Everything from the name of the hero (...) to all the business about the steps and the Tower of Babel, all that was in some early version of* Moon Palace.*"*[4]

As the *Moon Palace* project was steadily becoming more complex, the author decided to interrupt his work for a longer period of time:

> *"The funny thing is, as a young person I was trying to write prose, and I wrote a lot of it, but I was never satisfied with the results. Two of the novels I wound up finishing and publishing later I started very early on, in my early 20's,* In the Country of Last Things *and* Moon Palace. *Both of those books I worked a great deal on but never quite got a grip on either one. I put them aside and at a certain point decided I couldn't write prose, and I would just stick to writing poetry."*[5]

3 See Springer, *A Paul Auster Sourcebook*, pp. 69.
4 Ibid.
5 Interview with Paul Auster on 21st October 1996 for Worldguide (Stephen Capen): http://www.worldmind.com/Cannon/Culture/Interviews/auster.html [August 2006]

The final version of the novel, in which the protagonist's name as well as the first person narrative was decided upon, was developed between 1985 and 1988.
The diverse explicit and implicit intertextual references contained in *Moon Palace* have a number of literary sources. Among them are Sir Walter Raleigh's lyric poetry (ca. 1600), Shakespeare's tragedy *King Lear* (1608), *The Other World: The Comical History of the States and Empires of the Moon* (1649) by Cyrano de Bergerac, Charles Dickens's novel *David Copperfield* (1849), Hermann Melville's epic *Bartleby, the Bard* (1853), Fjodor Dostojewsky's *Crime and Punishment* (1866), Jules Verne's *Around the World in 80 days* (1872), Knut Hamsun's novel *Hunger* (1890) as well as Franz Kafka's *A Hunger Artist* (1924).[6]

Literary genre

The complex composition and the structure of *Moon Palace* allow this work to be classified under post-modernism, the cultural time period following modernism, which originated in the political, artistic and medical changes of the 1960s. Unlike modernism, however, post-modernism assumes reality in fragments. The resulting loss of orientation and reality, as well as the loss of the conventional awareness of history, are characteristics of post-modern literature and art. Post-modernism continues the sceptical perception of modernism but breaks with the elitist modern understanding of art. Instead, a mixture of traditional and new art concepts, means of expressions and structural principles are propagated[7]. Post-modernism particularly seeks to overcome the divide between 'High Culture' and 'Popular Culture'[8].

6 See Springer, pp. 35-37.
7 For more information on post-modern structural principles see also chapter 2.3.
8 Cf. Schweikle, Günther und Irmgard: *Metzler Literatur Lexikon. Begriffe und Definitionen*. Stuttgart: J.B. Metzlersche Verlagsbuchhandlung, 1990, pp. 438-439.

Nevertheless, because *Moon Palace* contains such diverse features, it is impossible to place it in just one type of category. Firstly, there is the 'rogue element', portrayed in the novel by the first person narrator, who describes the experiences and adventures from the point of view of a socially underprivileged person. Then, there are the elements of an adventure story, depicted by the chain of exciting events the main character finds himself involved in, but there is also the element of a 'coming-of-age' novel, as illustrated by the emotional, moral and spiritual development of the main character. At the same time, there is also a case for regarding this work as an artistic novel or, in view of Effing's or Solomon Barber's story, for arguing that it belongs to the Western genre.

2.2 Summary

Chapter One

The first-person narrator recalls his memories in the form of a summary. They take place in the summer of the year of the first moon landing. The narrator remembers a nihilistic and self-destructive phase that nearly cost him his life, had he not been saved by a girl called Kitty Wu. Afterwards, he worked for a wheelchair-bound man and discovered who his father was. Today, he views this part of his life as his rebirth.
In the autumn of 1965, the 18-year old narrator moves from Chicago to New York to study at Columbia University. He spends nine months in student accommodation before moving to an apartment on 112th West Street, where he spends three years. He decorates his flat with a farewell present from his Uncle Victor: Boxes with more than a thousand books which he uses to create "imaginary furniture" (p. 2). Uncle Victor's death in 1967 is a life-changing loss for the narrator, Marco Fogg.
Up to the age of 11, Fogg lived with his mother, Emily Fogg, in Boston. He can barely remember his mother, who died when she was just 29 or 30. She was only occasionally cheery, but most of the time she was dreamy and unhappy. Fogg grows up thinking that his father had died before he was born. As a child, he imagines him to be like "a dark-haired version of Buck Rogers, a space traveler who had passed into the fourth dimension and could not find his way back" (p. 4). After his mother's death in a traffic accident, he moves to Chicago to live with his uncle. His time at his uncle's has a lasting effect upon him. He is a clarinettist and, like all Foggs, he has "a penchant for aimlessness and reverie" (p. 5) and acts more like an older friend to Fogg. They both share a love of baseball. Victor stimulates Fogg's im-

agination, especially when he philosophizes about the meaning of names. For Victor, Marco Stanley Fogg's name

> *"proved that travel was in [his] blood, that life would carry [him] to places where no man had ever been before: Marco, naturally enough, was for Marco Polo, the first European to visit China; Stanley was for the American journalist who had tracked down Dr. Livingstone 'in the heart of darkest Africa'; and Fogg was for Phileas, the man who had stormed around the globe in less than three months"* (p. 6).

In fact, he had been named "Marco" simply because his mother had liked the name and "Stanley" after his grandfather who had moved to America at the turn of the century. The family's surname had originally been Fogelman, which immigration officials had shortened to Fog, and which had then later developed into Fogg.
At his new school, the children soon tease him about his surname. So Fogg starts initialing his work at the age of 15 with M.S. Fogg, whereby M.S. is the abbreviation for 'manuscript'. His uncle supports him in this as "'[E]very man is the author of his own life'" (p. 7). From that day on, Victor calls his nephew Phileas after the hero in Jules Verne's *Around the World in 80 days*. In 1958, Victor and Fogg move to Saint Paul in Minnesota because Victor has been offered a position as a music teacher there. However, they move back to Chicago after just one year.
Shortly after Fogg turns 14, Victor marries a plump mid-forty year-old alcoholic widow called Dora Shamsky. The first year of their marriage Fogg experiences as "infernal machine" (p. 9) which he escapes by going to boarding school in New Hampshire. The marriage is over after two years of his three year stay at the school. After completing boarding school, Fogg returns to his single uncle and is worried about his "physical lapses" (p. 10)

Fogg learns that his uncle's music group, the *Moonlight Moods*, where he played the clarinet have dissolved. In the meantime, Victor and his friend, Howie Dunn, have formed a new group, *the Moon Men*. The *Moon Men*'s plans to go on tour through the West of America prompt Victor to give Fogg a few farewell gifts: his collection of 1492 books, his collection of baseball autographs as well as a suit. Fogg moves to New York to study at Columbus University.

During his first year at university, Fogg tries to fit in. He fashions himself as the "sublime intellectual, the cantankerous and opinionated future genius, the skulking Malevole who stood apart from the herd" (p. 15). Outwardly, he distinguishes himself from his fellow students by his uncle's tweed suit, which he wears to stay spiritually connected to him. In his second year, he declines a house share with his friend, David Zimmer, as he prefers to live alone. On 14th June 1966, he moves into an apartment on West 112th Street which he furnishes with his uncle's 76 boxes of books. It is not until he makes "a singular discovery" (p. 16) that he begins to feel at home in the dismal attic studio apartment: the neon sign of a Chinese restaurant, Moon Palace the words of which "fill the view from his window onto Broadway in bright neon letters. The sight of this leads Fogg not only to gain control over his fears. He feels that by the neon sign his bare and grubby room had been transformed into a site of inwardness, "an intersection point of strange omens and mysterious, arbitrary events." (p. 16)

When Fogg turns 20, his uncle writes him a letter informing him that the *Moon Men* have broken up. He invites his depressed uncle to move from Boise, Idaho to New York with him. His uncle accepts but dies of a heart attack in Boise, which Fogg learns about over the phone from a policeman named Neil Armstrong. Fogg pays off Victor's debts and arranges the funeral. He is buried next to his sister, Fogg's mother.

In his grief over his uncle's death he is repulsed by society. Despite his financial problems, he decides not to apply for a grant, nor to find a job and escapes into nihilism. He reads Victor's books randomly but keenly, and they start to coin his understanding of the world around him. Between 1967 and 1969, his financial strains force him to sell the books he has read. Consequently, Fogg's apartment is emptied as every disappearing box destroys the imaginary furniture (the bed, chairs and desk). Fogg experiments with his state of mind. He observes the consequences his self-destructive actions have on his existence through the eyes of a philosopher: "I could follow the progress of my own dismemberment. Piece by piece, I could watch myself disappear." (p. 24)

The narrator reflects on the late 1960s – "'[t]hose were difficult days for everyone, of course. I remember them as a tumult of politics and crowds, of outrage, bullhorns and violence. By the spring of 1968, every day seemed to retch forth a new cataclysm. There were half a million soldiers in Vietnam (...) even the smallest thoughts were contaminated by [the Vietnam war]." (p. 24)

Fogg is personally involved in the student protests. He is one of hundreds to get arrested on the "battleground" (p. 24) and "[his] suit was long gone. Battered by the soaking it had taken in Chicago". (p. 25) His own story stands "in the rubble of these days, and unless this fact is understood, none of it will make sense" (p. 25). His friends are startled by Fogg's new appearance, "work boots, blue jeans, flannel shirts, and a secondhand leather jacket from an Army surplus store" (p. 25). As his financial worries mount, he isolates himself more and more from his environment and even cancels his phone without any explanation. Instead he hides behind the excuse that the use of the telephone is "communication between ghosts" (p. 25) so that he "starts sounding like an anarchistic hermit, a latter day crank" (p. 26). As he struggles to make ends meet, he starts hallucinating. The sale of the last books - which coincides with the day of the first Moon Landing - frees him from his past. The now empty apartment allows him to feel calm and happy. During this time, he records his thoughts in a notebook. "[T]he act of doing nothing" (p. 31) does not make him feel guilty and despite being hungry he enjoys musing at the neon sign of Moon Palace.

On 1st August 1969, the climax of his material poverty forces him to finally give up on his solitude and he tries to get help from his friend David Zimmer. As it turns out, he has moved and his old flat has new tenants. They are a mixture of students and artists, who Fogg meets over Sunday breakfast, among them is also the 20 year-old Chinese girl, Kitty Wu. At the sight of the rich offerings on the breakfast table, Fogg is overcome with a hunger attack and he devours everything that is put in front of him. He describes Cyrano de Bergerac's *The Other World: The Comical History of the States and Empires of the Moon* as a factual report. Kitty kisses him when he leaves.

On 13th August, Fogg receives his second eviction notice. He has no prospects and the only comfort he has is his uncle's clarinet. After dropping the last two eggs, he decides to go for a meal at Moon Palace, which he does not enjoy. He recalls the Elizabethan lyric poet Raleigh's last thoughts before his execution and equates his personal situation with it: *"My brains are broken"* (p. 42). He vegetates in his flat ignoring any knocking on the door. He receives a letter telling him to attend a physical examination for the military on 16th September, but because of his mental state he ignores it and puts it into Victor's clarinet case. The caretaker demands Fogg's immediate eviction and is appalled by what he sees: "Just a lot of bones" (p. 45). Fogg leaves his flat at the end of August 1969.

Key words/ important passages
"Every man is the author of his own life" (p. 7); 1492 books (p. 12); "Everything works out in the end, everything connects" (p. 13); "an intersection point of strange omens and mysterious, arbitrary events." (p. 16); "why does the American West look so much like the landscape of the moon?" (p. 32)

Chapter Two
Fogg recalls his life at the time of his eviction, but also includes details which he discovers only later: After finding the caretaker instead of Fogg in his flat, Kitty alerts his friend David Zimmer and they go out to look for him. Leaving his luck to chance, Fogg just starts walking. He avoids the area of Upper Broadway where he might meet people he knows. His pride and feelings of shame allow him to momentarily understand his situation. "A part of me was appalled by what I had allowed to happen to myself" (p. 49). With around 16 to 20 dollars in his pocket he decides to travel South. He spends the first couple of hours at the cinema with other homeless people. Coincidentally, the film *Around the World in 80 Days* is on and he interprets this as a sign of fate as he had watched this film eleven years previously with Uncle Victor. He finally becomes consciously aware of his situation: "I had turned myself into a nothing, a dead man tumbling head-first into hell." (p. 52) After leaving the cinema he decides to find a place to sleep and settles for Central Park. His frame of mind is dominated by extreme mood swings. He enjoys the solitude of the morning, the park becomes his "sanctuary (...) a refuge of inwardness against the grinding demands of the streets" (p. 55). Fogg experiences unexpected events like the kindness of a woman going for a walk who gives him five dollars. He lives off the rubbish the park visitors leave behind. As he becomes weaker, his fear of the streets increases. To get back on his feet

he interprets his life as *the American Way of Life*. He is "living proof that the system [has] failed" (p. 60). His continuous reflections mean that he never gets bored, as he later points out to Kitty and Zimmer (p. 60). From a discarded newspaper he learns of the decline of his favourite baseball team, Chicago Cubs, and applies this to his own decline.
When the weather gets worse, Fogg is exposed to wind and rain. He goes to the local library to shelter from the rain, but he soon has to leave because his clothes start smelling as they begin to dry. As a result, he becomes ill, develops a high temperature, and seeks refuge in a cave; his weight drops to 112 pounds. Two or three days later, whilst hallucinating about Moon Palace, he is found by Kitty Wu and David Zimmer.

Key words/ important passages
"I learned that there were people who loved me" (p. 49); "the one thing powerful enough to negate the laws of gravity" (p. 49); "I began to notice that good things happened to me only when I stopped wishing for them" (p. 57); "Causality was no longer the hidden demi-urge that ruled the universe; down was up, the last was the first, the end was the beginning" (p. 61); "reality was a yo-yo, change was the only constant" (p. 61); dream of Indians (pp. 68)

Chapter Three
Fogg stays in David Zimmer's flat for over a month. During this time, Kitty visits him regularly for a few minutes. It does not dawn on Fogg that she might feel more than pity for him, "It was somewhat strange, after all, that a person who had spent three weeks turning the world upside down to find me should suddenly act with such reserve the moment I was found" (p. 70). Zimmer proves to be a true friend who takes care of him and

shares his meager belongings without expecting anything in return. However, he does make sure Fogg knows that he thinks his behaviour was "grotesque", "unhinged" and "asinine" (p. 71) as he could have turned to him for help beforehand. Fogg discovers that his retreat into isolation was not an act of bravery but cowardice and feels "nothing but remorse" (p. 71). He knows that he has to start again in order to make up for the damage he has caused, to "accomplish something in the world" (p. 71).

A day before his physical examination for military service on 16th September 1969 he finds the letter again. Had he forgotten about it, he might have been arrested. Still weak, he manages to go to the appointment, assisted by David Zimmer, and is examined for the first time since his recovery: he is still so anemic and haggard that the doctor has trouble finding a vein. In his "new period of potential sainthood" (p. 76) he answers the psychiatrist's questions truthfully and defends his attempt of self-destruction. To his relief he is deemed unfit (p. 79).

At the end of the month the recovering Fogg is nearly back to normal. Every evening, he and Zimmer go out to a bar to watch baseball games to relax. It is during one of these evenings that Zimmer tells him about Kitty's love for him and about her life.

Fogg realises that he is becoming more and more of a burden for his friend and decides to look for a job to reimburse him. Zimmer has been commissioned to translate a text into French and Fogg offers to do it for him, and "for the first time in months [he] began to feel there was a purpose to [his] life again" (p. 88). During a walk in the park in October he bumps into Kitty Wu but as he is deeply engrossed in the translation, he only notices her when she sits down next to him. Fogg is overwhelmed by her at first but feels immediately at ease in her company. They hit it off straight away. They go back to Zimmer's flat where they become intimate. Fogg's life finally begins to return to normal.

He spends the days translating and the evenings with Kitty. He reminisces about this period of his life describing the romance as "erotic mysticism" (p. 93).

At the end of October the translation is finished. After submitting the transcript, he pays off his debts and takes Zimmer and Kitty out for dinner at *Moon Palace*. In a fortune cookie he finds "'The sun is the past, the earth is the present, the moon is the future'" (p. 94). He starts looking for a job the next day and comes across a vacancy on the student's notice board: An older wheelchair-bound gentleman looking for a companion, daily walks and easy secretarial tasks expected and offering 50 dollars, as well as bed and board. Fogg sees an opportunity to move out of Zimmer's flat and closer to Kitty; so he calls the number advertised. A mere two hours later, he meets his future employer, Thomas Effing, at his home and is offered the position.

Key words/ important text passages

Fogg lacks mediocrity; he moves from one extreme to the other, "From total selfishness, I resolved to achieve a state of total selflessness" (p. 71).

> *"(...) and every day we struggle against these shocks and accidents in order to keep our balance. Two years ago, for reasons both personal and philosophical, I decided to give up the struggle. (...) I thought that by abandoning myself to the chaos of the world, the world might ultimately reveal some secret harmony to me, some form or pattern that would help me to penetrate myself." (p. 78)*

Chapter Four

Fogg describes his first meeting with Thomas Effing on 1st November 1969. He perceives this 86-year old man as the most fragile and oldest person he has ever seen. Crouched in his wheelchair Effing appears to Fogg "walled off, remote, sphinxlike in its impenetrability" (p. 96). To add to this, Effing is blind. Rita Hume, who greets Fogg at the door, has been Effing's carer and his housekeeper for nine years. Despite her curiosity, Fogg perceives her as endearing. Mrs Hume soon becomes an ally against his eccentric employer. One of Effing's first peculiarities is when he prophesies that Fogg will learn about fear in his services.

Effing demands two things of Fogg: a strong voice (to read to him daily) and muscle strength (to push Effing on his long walks through town). He also tells Fogg that he will soon grow to hate him but that everything has a purpose which Fogg should not judge.

On the evening after his interview, Fogg says goodbye to David Zimmer. The narrator reports that "[a]s chance would have it" (p. 102), he was to see his friend again thirteen years later. In the spring of 1982 he runs into him by chance in Manhattan. Zimmer has published a study on French film and has turned into a demure family father. He informs the reader that it was this chance meeting that inspired him to write his book.

Fogg is employed at Mr. Effing's as "a sympathetic companion, a person to break the monotony of his loneliness" (p. 103). Fogg quickly realises that Effing is "a sharp customer" (p. 104). He develops an ambivalent relationship to him: Sometimes, he finds him repulsive, then at times he "felt that he was trying to pass on some mysterious and arcane knowledge to [him]" (p. 105). It is Kitty who convinces him to stay on after some frustrating experiences (amongst them Effing's disgusting table manners and his swearing).

The readings are - as everything with Effing - consciously chosen: They serve the purpose of exploring certain subject matters. The daily routine is strictly regulated into the reading of travel books from all ages and long walks during which Fogg has to describe the surroundings in detail. Fogg has to learn not to take anything for granted, but to see it for its originality. He passes through "a stage of intense alarm" (p. 119). During this time Fogg sees himself as "a monk seeking illumination" and Effing as the "hair shirt, the whip I flayed myself with" (p. 120).

At the end of March/beginning of April the walks get longer and are complemented by field guides. By mid-December Effing has Fogg swapping the travel guides for newspapers. He is interested in all kinds of news but takes a particular interest in obituaries. This marks a turning point in Effing's and Fogg's relationship, as he starts referring to "our project" (p. 124) and declares that reading the obituaries is a kind of research in preparation for his own, which Fogg is to write. He tells Fogg that he is certain his time is up and lets him into the secrets of his past: 52 years previously he had already been declared dead and an obituary had been posted for him. However, his name then had been Julian Barber and he had been a great American painter.

At this point, Effing interrupts his story and does not pick up the thread the next day. Instead, he tells Fogg about a former acquaintance whom he describes as "a midget" and "poor buggar" (p. 127) and who is called Ralph Albert Blakelock. He used to travel into the Wild West to the Indian tribes and was "one of the greatest men we've ever had" (p. 128). Towards the end of his life, he had gone mad and wandered around New Jersey in an Indian costume before he was committed. Blakelock's painting, *Moonlight*, was sold for the highest price that a painting by a living artist had ever been sold for. When Fogg admits to not knowing this artist, Effing is outraged and immediately orders him to go to *Brooklyn Museum* to see the painting. He tells Fogg that on his way there he must not think and he must keep his eyes shut. Through this experiment Fogg learns "what it meant to be blind" (p. 132).

After arriving at the museum, Fogg goes straight to this painting: it appears to him like the lost idyll of the West, of the Indians before their world was destroyed by the white people. He does some research on Blakelock and discovers that Effing was telling the truth. He learns that Blakelock created his paintings in New York's Central Park in the 1870s and that he concentrated on painting moonlight landscapes. Contrary to his expectations, Effing does not mention the painter again the next day but instead continues the story of his life. He starts by mentioning another landscape painter of the time, Thomas Moran, who had inspired him at a young age. Then he goes into his family background. Julian Barber, who later became Effing, grew up in Shoreham/Long Island where Tesla, a scientist who was Edison's rival, had built the *Wardenclyffe Tower* in 1901/1902. Tesla, whom he had known since he was young, had been caught between genius and madness. When Julian met him in Shoreham at the age of 17, he just looked straight through him. It was a humiliating experience for Effing/Barber because for the first time it made him aware of his own non-importance, but at the same time it also made him aware of his freedom. This led him to go against his father's wishes, who was a successful businessman on Wall Street, and became a painter. When Effing was 22/23, his father died and he inherited his vast wealth. Decades later, in 1939/1940, after returning to the USA from France, where he had spent 20 years after being presumed dead, he met Tesla in a park in New York by chance. The celebrated genius, Tesla, had turned into a destitute mad homeless person. Effing took his revenge on the scientist's humiliating gaze by embarrassing him with a donation.
After his account of this era, Effing turns his thoughts to Thomas Moran again, who had inspired him to travel to the American West. In 1916, a 33-year old Barber who had recently been

unhappily married to Elizabeth Wheeler decided to give his paintings a new inspiration. He took Edward Byrne, the son of a friend, with him. The night before they left, his wife insisted on her husband's duty, the consequences of which he does not find out about for another 30 years. In April 1916, Effing and Byrne took the train to Salt Lake City, where they hired a man named Jack Scoresby as their guide into the wilderness. Scoresby, who showed nothing but contempt for the city dwellers, ended up being responsible for Byrne's death. As the three were about to climb a steep mountain trail, Byrne fell and severely injured himself. When Effing insisted on taking care of the dying man, Scoresby abandoned them in the wilderness. Effing was confronted by death and it drove him insane. He tells Fogg that he is the first person to hear this story.

Key word/important passages
"There are no coincidences (...) If they're strong enough, a man's thoughts can change the world around him." (p. 101), Fogg's chance meeting with David Zimmer in 1982 which inspires him to write a book (p. 102); Fogg learns how to see and describe accurately, reflections about what he actually sees (pp. 117-122); Indian motif, Ralf Blakelock (p. 127); Fascination with the moon (p. 133); Julian Barber's main motive as painter: "the force of light when it hits the eye." (p. 145)

Chapter Five
Fog and Effing work on his obituary for several weeks. During this time Fogg fills several notebooks, about 20 to 30 pages per night, writing down information Effing gives him.
Fogg continues Effing's life story. At first, Julian Barber/ Effing's half-hearted attempt to escape from the canyon failed. He was held back by feelings of guilt and decided to die. On the morn-

ing of the 4th day, he stumbled across a cave which surprisingly contained a complete household consisting of a table, chairs, an oven and a shelf full of tins – enough to last a year. On the bed, he found the body of a man who had been shot and so he decided to assume this man's identity. Despite this happy coincidence, it took Effing months to become accustomed to the solitude. After some time, he decided in a moment of madness to stay in the cave until he was presumed dead. In order to survive on the contents of the tin cans for as long as possible, he started rationing. Shortly after, he was overcome with a frenzy of inspiration and completed nearly 40 paintings. He put his newly found inspiration down to two things: firstly, the fact that he was only painting for himself and that nobody was ever going to see these works of art and secondly, the limited amount of time he had to do them before running out of materials. Effing recognized that "[i]t was a method of understanding, a way of penetrating the world and finding one's place in it" (p. 166). In his painting frenzy, he even started painting on the furniture and the cave's south wall. When he ran out of painting material in mid-winter, he started filling his notebooks; these were full by mid-February but by this time he had become so accustomed to the solitude that "little by little the world had become enough for him" (p. 168).

At the end of March, a clown-like Indian called George Ugly Mouth came to the cave and assumed him to be Tom, the recluse who had killed and whose identity Effing had taken on. Effing found out that the real Tom had been involved with the criminal activities of the Gresham brothers, a gang of bandits. He drew the conclusion that it was they who had killed him and that there was a likely chance that they might return at the end of spring.

Effing's life changed from then on. He was permanently on the lookout and suffered because of this. Some time during mid-May they arrived: while the three of them were making themselves comfortable in the cave, Effing hid and waited for them to get tired. Then, he managed to surprise and shot them. He did not feel any guilt at this. Effing found 20,000 dollars in the saddlebags and a few other valuable items and decided to keep them and to leave the cave with his pictures, "the tomb in which he had buried his past" (p. 178). He blocked the entrance to the cave with stones and branches.

It takes Barber/Effing and Fogg two weeks to record this part of Effing's life. Even though Effing's story has dreamlike elements to it, Fogg refuses to disbelieve it because of the frankness Effing displays in telling it. The meetings with Effing double in length. It is only the evenings with Kitty that give Fogg the strength to escape from the claustrophobic atmosphere of the house.

After leaving the cave, Effing wandered through the desert for a few days before he came across the town of Bluff and went back to Salt Lake City. Then on to San Francisco where he worked on building up his new identity as Thomas Effing. He used the Gresham brothers' money to build his new life. As time progressed, his new identity came under threat as he attended social events. Feelings of guilt drove him to brothels, opium and gambling dens where he gambled away a third of his money.

One night on his way home from Chinatown, he was hit over the head. He fell and slid down the street until his fall was broken by a lamppost. His spine was broken and he was paralyzed from then on. He considered this to be his punishment for killing the criminal gang and for faking his death in the desert. He never found out who administered the blow. After a recuperation period of nine months, he left America in September 1920 and moved to France. Fogg is not as fascinated by Effing's description of living in France as he was in the beginning which is why he does not make any notes on Effing's friendship with Pavel Shum, Fogg's predecessor (see p. 186). Effing, too, feels that his life from 1939 onwards could be described in general sentences as he has not got much time left. Fogg has to write three versions in the following days; one shortened version for the newspaper, one detailed version entitled *The Secret Life of Julian Barber* to be published in an art magazine and one revised version of the complete notes. At the beginning of March, the work is completed. The next day, Fogg finds three books by a historian named Solomon Barber on his bed. On the basis of the dates given, Fogg assumes that Solomon Barber may be Effing's son, the product of his last night with Elizabeth Wheeler. Effing explains to Fogg that he came upon his name by chance but, after Shum had collected some data on him, he had been at once certain that he was his son.

During the time when Shum was researching information on Solomon Barber (post 1947) he found out that Barber was teaching in Mid-West America. The historian was born in 1917 in Shoreham/Long Island. His father, a painter, had died a long time before in Utah and his mother in 1939. As a young university lecturer, Solomon Barber had been involved in a scandal, an affair with a female student and this had had severe consequences for his career. According to Effing, Solomon Barber was a "fat, childless, unmarried, broken-down wreck, a walking dirigible disaster" (p. 192). Out of pity he decides to leave his fortune to him. Effing instructs Fogg to pass on to Solomon a detailed version of his life story after his death. He wants his son, whom he has never contacted, to at least know about his past.

Effing prophesies his own death and tells Fogg that he will die on 12th May, in two months' time. Effing's reading becomes incoherent and he becomes lethargic which lasts for about three weeks. Then Effing suddenly declares euphorically at breakfast that he has "the perfect plan" (p. 195): With Fogg's help he wants to give 20,000 dollars in cash - exactly the sum he obtained 52 years previously from the gang - to the needy and homeless in order to clear his debt. Despite Mrs. Hume's and Fogg's objections he insists upon it. During the first couple of days, everything goes to plan and the reaction of the recipients is as expected. On the ninth evening, however, Fogg forces Effing to stay at home because it is raining by threatening to resign. On their next trip out, they meet the black comedian, Orlando, who turns the world upside down. Despite the sunshine, he pretends that it is raining whilst holding a broken umbrella. It is this act of imagination that Effing imitates on his last night: despite an impending thunderstorm, he takes the torn umbrella Orlando has given him and enthusiastically subjects himself to the pouring rain. It is only then that Fogg understands that he wants to die. Infected by Effing's madness, he helps him to distribute the last notes.

After their return, Effing does not leave the house again. He has caught pneumonia and insists on dying in his own bed; Fogg spends every day with him. Since the storm, Fogg worships him "as if I were his own flesh and blood" (p. 211).

In the end he manages to die at "12:02" (p. 215). When he dies, an exhausted Fogg is out with Kitty. Effing is cremated. Fogg, Mrs Hume, her brother Charlie Bacon and Kitty scatter his ashes in New York harbor. Fogg carries out Effing's instructions and sends Solomon Barber the detailed manuscript of Effing's life story by post. Before her departure to Florida, Mrs. Hume gives Fogg Effing's goodbye present of over 7000 dollars in cash.

Key words/important passages

Effing: Effing recognizes that "[i]t was a method of understanding, a way of penetrating the world and finding one's place in it" (p. 166); the comedian Orlando who brings non-existent things to life (p. 203); Effing's final act, Learish insanity (p. 207);

Effing denies the existence of rain (p. 207), "It's mind over matter, Fogg. We've finally done it! We've cracked the secret of the universe!" (p. 208)

Chapter Six

After Effing's death, Fogg experiences a very positive time thanks to his unexpected windfall, *"a human paradise"* (p. 222) which lasts for eight or nine months. In mid-July 1970, he and Kitty move into a disused warehouse in Chinatown. Kitty finds a job while Fogg takes care of the household. Effing/Barber's obituary is not published in the newspapers as they do not believe his story and have forgotten about the mystery of his disappearance. Fogg relishes his "days in splendid indolence" (p. 226). By chance, he stumbles across Tesla's autobiography, *My Inventions*, dated 1919 in an antiques shop. In it he discovers a phrase about how the moon is the future, near enough the same phrase he had found in his fortune cookie a year previously in Moon Palace.

In September 1970, around four months after Effing has passed away, Fogg gets a letter from Solomon Barber. He thanks him for his efforts and asks to meet him in New York. On a Friday afternoon in October they meet in the foyer of the Warwick Hotel. Fogg is surprised at Barber's appearance as Effing had been lean and undersized. Barber is "immense, monumental in his bulk, a pandemonium of flesh heaped upon flesh" (p. 228). Barber starts off by asking him about a former student of his, Emily Fogg from Chicago, who he lectured in the 1940s and who Fogg strongly resembles.

At this point, Fogg antedates insights that only come to light ten months later when Solomon Barber is lying in hospital with a broken back. He does not find out until then that Barber had already recognized him as his son as soon as he saw him at the

Warwick Hotel. It had been Emily who Barber had spent the night with, the night on which Marco Fogg had been conceived, the night which had caused the scandal destroying Barber's career and to which Effing had alluded earlier (see p. 192). The student, Emily Fogg, had been caught in bed with her history lecturer by a cleaner and this had led to Barber being sacked and Emily fleeing to Chicago. Barber's career never recovered from this blow and he never recovered from Emily's rejection after she blamed him for having ruined her life. Despite the futility of trying to find her, he finally succeeded 13 years later only to discover that she had died. Emily had taken the secret of her son to her grave.

Fogg outlines Solomon Barber's life story bit by bit in the same way that he has learned about it. His perceived repulsive appearance led Solomon to seek refuge in books from a young age. He finished High School at the top of his class and studied at Columbia University just as "his unwitting son would do twenty-nine years later" (p. 234). In 1944, he finished his PhD on Bishop Berkeley and the Red Indians and began teaching at Ohio University. He was a popular teacher and Emily Fogg fell in love with him. After losing his job as well as Emily, he was unable to focus on anything for four months. First, he went to Cleveland where he decided to throw himself from a building, but then he changed his mind and compensated by overeating. He expanded more and more and to top it off, he started losing his hair. At this point, he decided to shave it all off and to wear extravagant hats. He earned a living from jobs at small and meaningless colleges in the West and Mid-West and from his publications. He is no longer just "the fattest professor anyone had ever seen, but also The Man Who Wore Hats" (p. 238).

Fogg interrupts the narration of his father's life story by speculating about three possible chance meetings Effing, Solomon Barber and his Uncle Victor may have had, based on his researches. The first could have taken place at the World Exhibition in 1939 in New York, which Barber and Victor had visited. A second meeting may have taken place in Lincoln Park/ Cleveland in 1946, and the third in Saint Paul/ Minnesota which Victor had left abruptly in 1959. This event happened to coincide with a letter Solomon Barber wrote to Victor, after recognizing his surname, in which he asked about Emily. Fearing that he may lose the boy, Victor decided to leave Minnesota rapidly. All the emotions about his uncle come flooding back. He finds it difficult to accept that his uncle may have prevented him from meeting his father.

At Fogg's and Barber's first meeting at the Warwick Hotel, they mainly talk about Effing. Fogg is fascinated by his intellect and charm and forgets about his appearance. They both tell each other their life-stories. Barber tells Fogg how his mother, Elizabeth Wheeler, went mad after her husband's disappearance and had to be sectioned, which is why he grew up without a mother. He dealt with his absent father by writing a fiction about his disappearance when he was 17. Barber later sends Fogg the manuscript of his novel, *Kepler's blood*. It is a mixture of Wild West meets Science Fiction and set 40 years previously, in the 1870s, "but otherwise the story follows almost directly from the few things that Barber had managed to learn about his father" (p. 247). A thirty-five year old artist, John Kepler, says goodbye to his wife and young son and leaves his Long Island home for a six-month trek through Utah and Arizona to "discover a land of marvels, a world of wild beauty and ferocious colour" (p. 247). On his travels, he gets hurt and is saved by Native Americans who call themselves 'the Humans' and whose ancestors originate from the Moon. In this fantasy world, 'The Humans' live in harmony with 'The Others' until "The Wild Men took out their thunder-and-lightening sticks and killed them" (p. 249).

Kepler learns their language and believes that he can recognize elements of English in it. The legend of the moon must have originated in Utah as "nowhere in the world (...) does the earth look more than like the moon" (p. 251). Kepler has been saved by the Humans "to become a father to the new generation" (p. 251).
15 years on, John Kepler junior's mother has died and he decides to track down his missing father. He travels to Utah and stumbles across the 'Human's' settlement in the rocks. He recognizes his father but when he is rejected by him, he seeks revenge. In the dead of night he stabs him and flees, not having noticed the only witness, his half-brother, Jocomin. To avenge his father and save his species, Jocomin learns how to transform himself.
Years later, he ventures into the World of 'The Wild Men' calling himself Jack Moon and manages to find his half-brother, who by this time is married and has children, in New York. To take revenge, he kidnaps John Kepler Junior's 6 year-old son and returns to his tribe. However, they have disappeared and so he takes the boy on as his own. He transforms himself into a woman and has twins, who are destined to become the ancestors of a new 'Human' tribe. In the meantime, John Kepler Junior has been looking for his son in New York and finds the trace of Jack Moon. He travels to Utah and kills a coyote while "a full moon is poised dramatically in the sky" (p. 255) without realizing that it is in fact his own son who had transformed himself into the animal. Following this, 3 other coyotes tear him to pieces.
Fogg sees his father's work as a dramatic psychological attempt as "it demonstrates how Barber played out the inner dramas of his early life" (p. 256).
After renarrating *Kepler's Blood*, Fogg returns to Barber's autobiography. After his mother's death in 1939, he has a last chance to find out something about his father through his Aunt Clara.

She tells him about the search for his father that lasted for 6 months and about his birth. His mother who had gone mad did not want to give birth to him. He was saved thanks to his height and weight. Solomon Barber decided to give Aunt Clara his parents' house and never to set foot in it again. Barber tells Fogg this story at the end of their meeting at Warwick Hotel in October 1970 and leaves with tears in his eyes.

One day in mid-January, Fogg receives a call from Solomon Barber, who in the meantime has moved to New York. He invites him and Kitty out. Barber has decided to find the cave his father stayed in and asks Fogg to help him find it. They develop a friendship, however, Fogg does not take Barber's idea of the expedition seriously and decides to talk him out of it.

During the next eight months, Fogg and Kitty's relationship takes a turn for the worse. At the end of March, Kitty discovers that she is pregnant and panics. Fogg wants to start a family with her but she decides to have an abortion. He reluctantly agrees to this at first but changes his mind once it's too late. Kitty too regrets her decision and Fogg "watched her suffer, and at a certain point he realises that he was enjoying it" (p. 274). When he finally "saw the ugliness and cruelty that were inside [him], [he] turned against [himself] in horror" (p. 274). Fogg leaves her, despite her pleas to stay.

Key words/important passages

Fogg in Chinatown: I "could not penetrate the meanings of the things I saw" (p. 223); Fogg imagines Julian Barber's lost paintings: "I had dreamed them for myself from his words, and as such they were perfect, infinite, more exact in their representation of the real than reality itself." (p. 226); Fogg discovers the same sentence he found in his fortune cookie in *Moon Palace* in Tesla's autobiography (p. 227); Solomon Barber's bald head is like a moon to the rest of his body: "it seemed right to him that the vast globe of his body should now have a moon to go with it." (p. 236); Solomon is a popular teacher despite his size (p. 238), "The mind can indeed be more powerful than the body" (p. 238), The role of chance:

> *"It was all a matter of missed connections, bad timing, blundering in the dark. We were always in the right place at the wrong time, the wrong place at the right time, always just missing each other, always just a few inches from figuring the whole thing out. That's what the story boils down to, I think. A series of lost chances. All the pieces were there from the beginning, but no one knew how to put them together."* (p. 243);

Solomon turns into Sol: sun and earth (p. 244)

Chapter Seven

After leaving Kitty, Fogg stays with Barber for the rest of the spring. He finds a job as a removal man to distract himself from his pain. Barber tries to mediate but is unsuccessful, and Fogg refuses to talk about the reason for the separation. Barber learns from Kitty that she has unintentionally broken Fogg's heart. The first person narrator puts his ruthless behavior down to his lack of kindness.

At the end of June 1971, Barber and Fogg go to the *White Horse Tavern* for a drink. It's the bar Fogg used to frequent with David Zimmer, and Barber reiterates his idea of retracing Effing's footsteps. This time Fogg agrees. They take two weeks to put their plan into action and decide to take a detour via Chicago and Minnesota, so that Fogg can see his mother and uncle's grave. The trip brings Fogg closer to Barber.

When they reach Westlawn Cemetary in Chicago, Barber is strangely depressed and they both start crying at Emily's and

Victor's graves. Overcome with emotion, Barber confesses that he is Fogg's father, to which Fogg reacts with blind rage and disgust. "Blind to everything around him, he lurched down the row of graves like some injured animal, howling and sobbing as I continued to scream at him" (p. 284). Suddenly, he loses his balance and falls into an open grave, breaking his spine. After going to hospital, Fogg spends the two months up to his death at his bedside. During this time, Barber, whose health seems to be improving, tells him about his unhappy affair with Fogg's mother and Fogg learns to accept him as his father. During his stay in hospital, Barber loses so much weight that even Fogg cannot deny their resemblance. Barber dies on 4th September 1971, having slimmed down to 210 pounds. In his desperation, Fogg calls Kitty to tell her about Barber's death. He begs her to take him back but she tells him that their separation was too much for her; it seems that she has found somebody else. Fogg buries his father next to his mother according to Barber's wishes. He uses the money he has inherited to find Effing's cave. With 13.000 dollars in his pocket, he sets off to the village called Bluff. Following Julian Baber's trail, he reaches the Navajo's trading post, Oljeto the word meant "moon in the water" (p. 295). They do not know a George Ugly Mouth there, but they recall the gang of the Gresham brothers who vanished over 50 years ago. Their hideout was high up in the mountains near Rainbow Bridge. However, the cave could no longer be reached by foot as everything had been flooded two years previously and now the site was known as Lake Powell. On hearing this, Fogg gives up. He hires a motorboat and rides around on Lake Powell disappointedly. Having returned to dry land, he discovers that his hire car with all his valuables has been stolen. He spends the night by the side of the road. Angry at his destiny, he starts walking westward for three months. He spends the nights out in the open until he reaches Laguna Beach/California on the Pacific Coast. He stands on the beach watching the rise of the moon.

Key word/important passages

> *"We would search, but we would not find. Only the going itself would matter, and in the end we would be left with nothing but the futility of our own ambitions. This was a metaphor I could live with, the leap into emptiness I had always dreamed of" (p. 279)*

Fogg recognizes his father:

> *"(...) and all of a sudden I realised that I was looking at myself (...) Once I became aware of this, once the truth of it was finally thrown up against me, I had no choice but to accept it. I was Barber's son, and I knew it now beyond a shadow of a doubt" (p. 288).*

2.3 Structure

The main character in *Moon Palace* is an uprooted individual who seeks to find himself in a reality which is dominated by absurdity and chance. As the supposed writer of 'his life story' Fogg writes it down in 1986, just after he has coincidentally met David Zimmer again:

> *"I have not seen or heard from him since [Spring 1982, meeting after 13 years], but I suspect that the idea to write this book first came to me after that meeting four years ago [Time of writing 1986!] at the precise moment when Zimmer vanished down the street and I lost sight of him again."* (p. 103)

The protagonist narrates the story, and, as such, he is naturally not omniscient. He can only guess at the other characters' feelings and thoughts by drawing his own conclusions through dialogue; they are therefore subjectively portrayed. The novel is characterised by a diverse and complex narrative which is divided into a main plot and several sub-plots. It consists of seven chapters of different lengths. The narrative is framed by the expository opening sequence and the final sequence which both contain the all-important moon motif.

2.3.1 Expository entry episode and final sequence

In the expository first passage, the narrator protagonist outlines the main subject, which is a major thread in the novel. He sets the scene (chronology, place, topic), as demonstrated in the following passage, before he commences the extraordinary account of his biography:

"It was the ***summer that men first walked on the moon*** *(chronological context: Summer of 1969).* ***I*** *was* ***very young*** *back then, but I did not believe there would ever be a future.* ***I wanted*** *to live dangerously,* ***to push myself as far as I could go, and then see what happened to me when I got there. As it turned out, I nearly did not make it*** *(Topic: Crossing of boundaries). Little by little, I saw my money dwindle to zero; I lost my apartment; I wound up living in the streets (Topic: Pure survival).* ***If not for girl named Kitty Wu, I probably would have starved to death*** *(Topic: Love/companionship vs. Life of solitude), I had met her by chance only a short time before, but eventually I came to see that* ***chance*** *(Topic: Chance) as a form of readiness , a way of saving myself through the minds of others.* ***That was the first part****. From then on, strange things happened to me. I took the job with the old man in the wheelchair. I found out who my father was (Topic: Quest for identity). I walked across the desert from Utah to California (Regional context: not confined to one place but transboundary, journeying westward). That was a* ***long time ago****, of course, but I remember those days well, I remember them as the* ***beginning of my life*** *(Concern: His biography)"* (p. 1).

The first person narrator reveals his name retrospectively. He begins by describing his New York apartment, which only consists of boxes of books, and goes on to explain the cause for his 'displacement' which was triggered by the death of his only relative, Uncle Victor: "My Uncle simply dropped dead one fine afternoon in the middle of April, and at that point my life began to change, I began to vanish into another world." (p. 3)
In the novel's final sequence, after having marched through the desert until he reached the Californian West Coast, Fogg is in a state of happiness after discovering that he has found the answer

to an important question: "(...) but the answer had already been formed in my steps, and I had only to keep walking to know that I had left myself behind, that I was no longer the person I had once been." (p. 297)
He reaches the Pacific Coast in Laguna Beach on 6th January 1972. Standing on the beach, he has reached "the end of the world" (p. 298) and decides: "This is where my life begins" (p. 298). He gazes over the ocean and watches the moon rise, "not turning away until it had found its place in the darkness" (p. 298).

2.3.2 Main plot

In the opening sequence, the reader is given a short autobiography of the life of the protagonist, Fogg, before being taken on a journey from Fogg's arrival in New York in 1965 (first chapter) through to his arrival on Laguna Beach/California on 6th January 1972 (chapter seven). For Fogg, the protagonist and narrator of the story, it is a journey of self-discovery, which begins against the background of the first moon landing (1969) and ends with his arrival on the Pacific Coast in 1972.

August 1969	Fogg is evicted from his apartment in New York and spends several weeks in Central Park
September	Fogg is rescued by David Zimmer and Kitty Wu.
1st November 1969–May 1970	Fogg works for Thomas Effing and learns about his life story. Effing dies.
12th May 1970	Fogg moves in with Kitty Wu.
June	Fogg meets Solomon Barber and learns about Barber's life story.
October	Barber has moved to New York.
January 1971	He informs Kitty and Fogg of his plan to find the hidden cave. Kitty becomes pregnant and Fogg reluctantly finances the abortion.
March	Fogg leaves Kitty and moves in with Barber.
around May	Fogg and Barber travel West. At
July	his family's grave, Fogg learns that Barber is his father. Solomon Barber dies.
4th September October 1971– 6th January 1972	Fogg marches through the desert until he reaches the Pacific West Coast. Whilst watching the rising of the moon, he decides that this is where his life should begin.

However, the line of the main plot is neither linear nor chronological, as this timeline suggests. The main plot is in fact constantly being interrupted by flashbacks and glimpses into the future which in themselves contain individual life stories (see

Kitty Wu's, Effing's and Barber's autobiographies) that relate back to the main plot.

2.3.3 Main plot and subplots

The intertwinement of the main plot with the various subplots that interrupt the storyline seemingly at random, not only makes the structure of the novel very complex, but also allows reality to be presented in a fragmented and ambiguous form.

Chapter 1:

Main plot: Events leading up to Fogg's breakdown

- Autumn 1965: An 18 year old Fogg comes to New York to study (p. 1)
- 14th June 1966: Fogg moves into the flat on 112th Street West (p. 2 and p. 11)
- Spring 1967: Uncle Victor dies (p. 2) Nihilism, increasing financial struggle (p. 22), hunger (p. 28), participation in student protests (p. 24)
- Summer 1967-20th July 1969: Gradual sale of Uncle Victor's books (p. 29 and p. 30)
- August 1969: Fogg meets Kitty Wu (p. 35), breakdown (p. 44), and eviction from his flat (p. 45)

Significance of these events: The narrator is concerned with telling his own life story. There is a link between his experiences and those of history (Vietnam War, student protests): "My own story stands in the rubble of those days, and unless this fact is understood, none of it will make sense." (p. 25)

Subplot: Fogg's family history (pp. 1-19)

- memories of his mother (and the supposed death of his father)

- 1958: his mother dies, the 11 year old Fogg goes to live with his Uncle Victor (p. 3)
- 1958-1965: Fogg's stay with Uncle Victor in Chicago (pp. 4-9)
- 1958-1959: year-long stay in Saint Paul/Minnesota and sudden return (p. 8, see also p. 241: Solomon Barber's letter to Uncle Victor.

Chapter 2:
Main plot: Fogg is homeless
- From end of August 1969: Fogg's time as a homeless person in Central Park, *'unexpected things'* (p. 56), reflections (p. 57), illness (p. 92)
- September 1969: Fogg is rescued by Kitty Wu and David Zimmer (p. 69)

Subplot: Kitty Wu searching for Fogg (pp. 47-49)

Chapter 3:
Main plot: recovery at David Zimmer's apartment; Fogg and Kitty Wu
- 16th September 1969: physical examination for military service (pp. 74-79)
- September-October 1969: position as translator (pp. 87-93), relationship between Fogg and Kitty (pp. 91-95)
- 31st October 1969: Fogg invites David and Kitty to the Moon Palace restaurant (p. 93)
- 1st November 1969: Fogg finds a position with accommodation at Thomas Effing's (p. 94)

Subplot: Kitty Wu's life story (pp. 83-84)

Chapter 4:
Main plot: Fogg's time at Thomas Effing's, Part I

- 1st November: Interview at Thomas Effing's (pp. 96-102)
- Fogg moves out of David Zimmer's apartment, last contact with David (p. 102)

[**Insertion**: Spring 1982: chance meeting with David Zimmer (p. 102)]

- From November 1969: Fogg at Effing's (pp. 103-158)
  Duties: reading, going for walks, spiritual exercises, observations (pp. 104-137), Nature and travel guides (p. 14, pp.107)
- Mid-December 1969: Start of the 'obituary project' (pp. 123-129)
  Assignment: Study of Blakelock's *Moonlight* painting (pp. 129-137)

Subplot: Thomas Effing/Julian Barber's life story (pp. 125-156)

- 1893: Effing's first encounter with Tesla in Shoreham (p. 138)
- 1900 (?): Tesla's humiliating gaze at Barber (pp. 142-144)

[**Insertion**: Summer 1939: last encounter with Tesla in New York (p. 143)]

- Spring 1916: Marriage to Elizabeth Wheeler, Effing is 33 (p. 146)
- From April 1916: Voyage into Utah's desert with E. Byrne; Guide Jack Scoresby (p. 148)
- August 1916: Byrne's death, madness, feelings of guilt (pp. 154-158)

Chapter 5:
Main plot: Fogg's time at Thomas Effing's, Part II

- December 1969-March 1970: Fogg works on Effing's obituary (p. 123, pp. 137, 146), evening meetings with Kitty (p. 179), Fogg creates three versions of Effing's life (p. 189)
- Beginning of March 1970: Fogg finds out about Effing's son, Solomon Barber (pp. 187)
- April 1970: Effing's plan: to clear his debts (p. 196)
- April 1970: Distribution of money, clearing his debts (pp. 199-206), Orlando episode (pp. 204)
- 12th May 1970: Effing dies of pneumonia, brought on by himself (p. 214)
- May 1970: Fogg sends the obituary to Solomon Barber (p. 216), Scattering of Effing's ashes in New York harbor, Fogg inherits 7000 dollars. (pp. 216-221)

Subplot: Effing's/Julian Barber's life story continued (pp. 156-192)

- August 1916: Byrne dies and Julian Barber disappears p.164
  New life as a hermit in a cave (pp. 165)
  New inspiration for the painter (pp. 165-167)
- March 1917: George Ugly Mouth disrupts the idyllic solitude (pp. 165-167)
- May 1917: The Gresham brothers are killed (pp. 174-176)
- Julian Barber/hermit 'Tom' crosses the desert (p. 180)
- He reaches San Francisco and calls himself Thomas Effing (p. 180)
- 1919: Opium-phase, his spine is broken, becomes paralyzed (pp. 182-184)
- September 1920: Flight to France (p. 185)
- Friendship with Pavel Shum (p. 186)
- Return to the USA (p. 186)
- Effing finds out by chance about his fatherhood (p. 190)

Chapter 6:
Main plot: Fogg and Solomon Barber
- From June 1970: Fogg's *'human paradise'* with Kitty in Chinatown (p. 222)
- September 1970: Solomon Barber's letter (pp. 228)
- October 1970: Meeting with Solomon Barber at the Warwick Hotel (pp. 229-230, pp. 243)
- January 1971: Solomon Barber's proposal of a *'desert tour'* on the tracks of Effing/Julian Barber, and Fogg's rejection of the idea (pp. 268-270)
- March-June 1971: Break-up with Kitty (pp. 271-274); pregnancy, abortion and separation

Subplot: Solomon Barber's life story (pp. 229-247, pp. 256-265) and Barber's novel, *Kepler's Blood* (pp. 246-256)
- June 1936: Barber's farewell speech at Shoreham High School (p. 234)
- Spring 1939: Barber's conversation with Aunt Clara (pp. 257-260)
- Up to 1940: Study at Columbia University, 1944: Dissertation (pp. 234)
- Spring 1946: Solomon Barber spends the night with Emily Fogg (pp. 231 and 232) Scandal, he loses Emily, his career is in ruins

[**Insertion**: Fogg imagines three possible chance meetings between Uncle Victor, Effing (grandfather) and Barber (father): 1939, 1946 and 1959 (pp. 239-240)]

Importance of the insertions:
Fogg is deeply affected by his father's life story (p. 242).

Fogg's fantasies:
Fogg interrupts his narrative and attempts to fit the imaginary meetings into the individual life stories: "I like to imagine them standing together in front of some exhibit (...) and then bumping into each other by accident (...) I can trick myself into believing that these things truly happened." (pp. 239) Despite his unemotional narrative (which is reflected in his avoidance of the word 'grandfather' and 'father') Fogg is deeply touched. His fantasies can therefore be interpreted as his wish for his family to be reunited.

Chapter 7:
Main plot: Fogg's ‚new' life

- From around May 1971: lives with Solomon Barber, works as a removal man, suffers from the breakup with Kitty
- End of June: Conversation between Barber and Fogg in the *White Horse Tavern*, decision to go exploring (pp. 278)
- Early July 1971: Start of the 'expedition' into Utah's desert (p. 281)
- July 1971: stopover at the family grave in Chicago/Minnesota (p. 282)
  Barber's emotional revelation
  Fogg discovers that Solomon Barber is his father
  Barber's accident, broken spine, two months in hospital (pp. 284)
- 4th September 1971: Solomon Barber dies (p. 289)
  telephone call with Kitty (pp. 290-291)
- Barber is buried in the Fogg's family grave, Fogg destroys the motel room (p. 293)
- Continues to search for Effing's cave, but fails to find it
- Loses car and money (pp. 295-296)

- Fogg spends three months walking to Laguna Beach
- 6th January 1972: Fogg stands on Laguna Beach watching the rising of the moon: New beginning (p. 298)

Subplot: ----------

Overview of the structure of *Moon Palace*

New York, Summer 1969	**August 1969**	**September – October 1969**	**November 1969**	**December 1969 – May 1970**	**May 1970 – May 1971**	**May 1971 – January 1972**
Events leading up to Fogg's breakdown	Fogg is homeless	Recovery at David Zimmer's apartment; Fogg and Kitty Wu	Fogg's time at Thomas Effing's, Part I	Fogg's time at Thomas Effing's, Part II	Fogg and Solomon Barber	Fogg's 'new' life
Main Plot ↕	Main Plot ↕	Main Plot ↕	Main Plot ↕	Main Plot ↕	Main Plot ↕	Main Plot ↕
Chapter 1	Chapter 2	Chapter 3	Chapter 4	Chapter 5	Chapter 6	Chapter 7
↕ Subplot	↕ Subplot	↕ Subplot	↕ Subplot	↕ Subplot	↕ Subplot	↕ Subplot
Fogg's family history	Kitty Wu searches for Fogg	Kitty Wu's life story	Thomas Effing/ Julian Barber's life story	Effing's/ Julian Barber's life story continued	Solomon Barber's life story and Barber's novel, *Kepler's Blood*	----

2.3.4 Structural elements

The structure of *Moon Palace* displays both traditional as well as modern features, which is typical of post-modern literature. The following summary gives an overview of the most important elements of the structure and their meaning for *Moon Palace*.

Elements of the structure and their meaning within *Moon Palace*

Fragmentation:

Certain storylines/objects are only recounted in fragments or are incomplete. It is up to the reader to fill in the gaps or to draw his own conclusions.

For example:

- allusions to historical events (i.e. The student protests and Fogg's unexplained arrest p. 24).
- Emily Fogg's sadness (p. 3) which the reader only understands once Solomon Barber has explained it.
- Effing's alleged or actual blindness.
- Random names of places and time.

Cyclic narrative:

Certain procedures, topics, motifs or character constellations are repeated.

For example:

- Kitty reports how she found Fogg's flat and knocked on the door (the process of her knocking on the door is described from Fogg's perspective: "She heard me talking to myself in there (the words were too muffled for her to make them out)", p. 48).
- The narrative becomes cyclical when Fogg reflects at his physical examination for military service on his activities during the student protest movement (see p. 74).

- Other themes include his search for his father, his journey to the West (an experience which is mirrored by Uncle Victor, Fogg, Julian Barber and Solomon Barber), and prosperity through inheritance.

Parallel events:
Strong parallels can be seen in the narrative between the life stories of the three main characters, which stresses the importance of family ties for *Moon Palace*.
Cycles and parallel events match the key theme of the moon and its regular phases. This constant stands in stark contrast to the other theme of chance.
For example:

- Fogg's near death experience in Central Park (as a result of his exposure to bad weather) and Effing's death which he brings upon himself (he exposes himself to a thunderstorm to catch pneumonia, pp. 208, p. 214).
- Both Effing and Solomon Barber fracture their spines (see p. 182 and pp. 284).
- Effing and Fogg both spend time living in a cave. Fogg feels connected to Effing: "In spite of the revulsion he sometimes inspired in me, I could not help thinking of him as a kindred spirit." (p. 179).
- Effing humiliates Tesla by giving him some money in the park (see p. 144), he repays 'this debt' by giving away money (see pp. 199); Fogg is given money by a passer-by (see pp. 56/57).

Metafiction (fiction about fiction):
The fictitious statements and/or elements that occur in *Moon Palace* are also an important feature of the structure. They serve to remind the reader that he is in fact reading a piece of fiction, and to direct his attention to the literary development of the novel.

For example:

- Uncle Victor's statement that "[e]very man is the author of his own life" (p. 7).
- Paul Auster's fictitious main character, Fogg, writes his own autobiography (see p. 103) following his time at Effing's ("I suspect that the idea to write this book first came to me after that meeting", p. 103).

⇨ **The story within a story**:

For example:

- Effing's/Julian Barber's autobiography.
- Solomon Barber's novel *Kepler's Blood.*

Intertextuality:

The novel contains a number of references to other literary persona and texts. Some of these have been adopted literally word for word.

For example:

- *Moon Palace* is full of allusions to obvious as well as subtle literary, philosophical and historical references (e.g. many characters or objects bear the names of philosophers or authors: Mrs. Hume, her brother, Charlie Bacon, the antiques dealer Chandler, the ship, S.S. Descartes).
- Shortly before his mental breakdown, Fogg identifies himself with the poet, Sir Walter Raleigh, before his execution, and over breakfast with the students he tells them about Cyrano de Bergerac.
- Fogg's explanation for his disconnected phone because "it's communication between ghosts" (p. 25) is a reference to Franz Kafka's letter to Milena from March 1922[9]. In it the

---

9 Franz Kafka: Briefe an Milena, published by Juergen Born and Michael Mueller, Frankfurt/Main: S. Fischer, 1986, p. 315.

Prague poet denotes all forms of communication via letters, phones etc as "communication between ghosts"[10].

- Effing is overcome by artistic inspiration in the cave (p. 165). This is a reference to Platon's allegory of the cave and relates to one of the novel's key themes: mind versus matter and perception vs. recognition.
- Effing's 'final act' alludes to Shakespeare's *King Lear* wandering on the heath after a storm, Effing is described "midget Lear" (p. 207) who has succumbed to the same madness as King Lear. See also chapter 2.5.

Intermediality:
This refers to the use of other forms of media in a novel, e.g. fine arts in a literary text.
For example:
In *Moon Palace*, art and literature are linked to each other by the mention of real as well as fictitious artists and their works, and also through the analysis of theoretical and art-historical problems.
After mentally preparing himself, Fogg interprets Blakelock's work, *Moonlight* (see pp. 128-135). R.A. Blakelock (1847-1919) was an American Romantic artist whose painting, *Moonlight*, is exhibited in New York's *Brooklyn Museum*[11].
The Theory of Art/aesthetics is a key theme in *Moon Palace*, e.g. Effing discovers "a method of understanding, a way of penetrating the world and finding one's place in it" (p. 166) and decides to leave everything to fate and be spontaneous.

---

10 See above.
11 http://en.wikipedia.org/wiki/Ralph_Albert_Blakelock

2.3.5 Leitmotifs

Moon Palace is full of themes and imagery which are intended to support the key theme of the quest for identity, but are in fact as ambiguous and unfinished as the key theme itself.
The main motifs are the following:

1) Moon, Frontier, journey into the unknown (East-West movement), Native Americans
The particular importance of the moon is already evident in the title. This is reflected in the novel's first sentence: "It was the summer that men first walked on the moon" (p. 1). The historical event of Man landing on the moon in the summer of 1969 firstly sets the novel firmly in a historical context, and secondly, it underlines its central theme: The **moon landing** is seen as a milestone in Man's history as it was the first time that man had left earth and crossed into another world. This theme is also mirrored in the American journey from East to West (see also Fogg's journey from New York via Utah to California/The West Coast) with its positive (American Dream, new frontiers, pioneers) as well as negative consequences (eradication of the Native Americans; see also Chapter 1.2 and 2.5). However, the theme of crossing into another world is extended to crossing 'boundaries', in particular, intellectual and social ones, as demonstrated in the following sentence of the opening scene:

> *"I was very young back then, but I did not believe there would ever be a future. I wanted to live dangerously, to push myself as far as I could go, and then see what happened to me when I got there. As it turned out, I nearly did not make it"* (p. 1).

This suggests that Man's desire to cross boundaries, as symbolized by the moon landing, can also be applied to the main character. In the course of his journey, which is governed by chance,

the moon motif is recurring (see p. 30) and the main character is intrigued by it (see p. 31).
Yet it is the **diversity of** this **moon motif** that is of particular interest for the structure of the novel: It stands for repetition, estrangement and familiarity, proximity and distance and as well as being the guiding star for lunatics. Hereby, it is also important to remember the moon's cultural significance. Due to its periodically changing form, it traditionally represents the feminine (as supposed to the self-luminous sun which is masculine) and on a psychological level is regarded as representing the unknown. This is the key to Auster's novel as Fogg learns temporarily how to live in another dimension, meaning to be 'in touch' with his subconscious and decides to live by it (see pp. 20). It is therefore important to analyse how this theme impacts on other motifs.

The importance of the moon motif in relation to other themes

Moon = sentimental feelings

The moon is a reference point for sentimental and romantic feelings. Fogg and other characters are fascinated by it.

For example:

- Fogg regards himself as an expert on the moon landing and space travel. He demonstrates this over breakfast with the students when he grandiloquently holds a speech on spiritual precursors of the moon landing (such as Cyrano de Bergerac, who wrote a book on his fictitious journey to the moon in 1649, which Fogg passes off as the real thing, see pp. 37-38 and the reason why Kitty refers to him as Cyrano, see p. 7).
- Fogg and Solomon Barber share an interest in the English mathematician and astronomer Thomas Harriot (1560-1621) who is said to have been the first person to see the moon through a telescope (see p. 268 and 277).

- Uncle Victor (whose band is called *Moonlight Moods*, p. 5, and later *The Moon Men*, p.11), the artist Blakelock, whose painting is entitled *Moonlight*, Effing (who admires him), and finally Solomon Barber (who wrote a novel about people who originated from the moon in *Kepler's Blood*) are all characterized and linked to each other by their love of the moon.

Moon = symbol of a paradox reality
The moon is the symbol of a paradox reality which consists of change/chance and constancy/correlation. Reality is experienced in fragments and stands for the universality of the world and Man: Fogg's reality is ambivalent, unsettled and affected by chance. However, when he reflects about the moon, he gains momentary insights into their correlation and constancy (see p. 32).

Moon Palace = harmony and universality
The Chinese restaurant *Moon Palace* initiates feelings of harmony in a chaotic and fragmented reality.
For example:
- The sight of the bright neon letters of the Chinese restaurant, Moon Palace, help Fogg settle into his dismal apartment. Thinking of the moon gives him the feeling of stability despite having been uprooted: "They were magic letters, and they hung there in the darkness like a message from the sky itself" (p. 16). It is in the *Moon Palace* where Fogg celebrates his "return to the land of the living" (p. 94).

Moon = (endangered) myth
In the Middle Ages through to modern times, the moon has been perceived as a sort of barrier between the Kingdom of Heaven and the earthly world. The moon landing has destroyed

that myth, which scares Fogg.

For example:

- Fogg views the moon landing in a critical light as he sees it as the destruction of a myth:

  "I saw the two padded figures (...) planting a flag in the eye of what had once been the goddess of love and lunacy. Radiant Diana (...). Then the president spoke. (...) he declared this to be the greatest event since the creation of man" (p. 30).

- In Fogg's opinion, the moon landing has distanced Man from paradise: "Since the day he was expelled from Paradise, Adam had never been this far from home" (p. 30).
- Even Fogg's caretaker shares this opinion (see p. 45).
- In Fogg's feverish dream, the neon letters of the Moon Palace restaurant transform in his conscience. It is an attempt to kick-start his instinct of self-preservation in the light of his self-destruction: "The two os had turned into eyes, gigantic human eyes that were looking down at me with scorn and impatience." (p. 68)

Journey to the moon = symbol of journey into the unknown

The journey to the moon is a central theme in the novel which can be interpreted as the journey of life. The repeated journeys to the (unknown) American West help the characters gain a new perspective on their lives and their identities.

For example:

- Uncle Victor's journey to Western America; Fogg's and Kitty's 'journey' to New York to study at Columbia University (named after the explorer Christopher Columbus); the 'inspirational' journeys of the artist, Thomas Moran (1837-1926), Blakelock and Julian Barber (see p. 145); Solomon

Barber and Fogg's journey to Chicago (when they discover that they are father and son) and finally Fogg's march to the Pacific Coast.

- Even Fogg's choice of literature on his journey is of significance (*Prester John*, p. 108).

The Moon and the Native American motif; Blakelock's *Moonlight* – lost harmony through the eradication of the Native Americans

The themes of the moon and the Native Americans are the key to the theme of the quest for identity. The characters find their identity by meeting their ancestors and through exploring their family and cultural roots. Their investigation can also be seen in a cultural-historical context: as the Native Americans are part of the American national identity, the novel appears to allude to America's loss of cultural harmony (the key idea of American society being that all cultures live in peace and harmony) and points the finger of blame at America. In this context, the topic of guilt and atonement is brought up.

For example:

- Fogg's second feverish dream is about Native Americans. This dream symbolizes Fogg's 'unconscious' perception of himself as an 'urban adventurer', as a survivor of a lost idyll: "It was 350 years ago, and I saw myself following a group of half-naked men through the forests of Manhattan" (p. 68).
- R.A. Blakelock, the artist who painted *Moonlight*. After studying the lost idyll of the Native Americans, he became a lunatic.
- In Solomon Barber's novel, *Kepler's Blood*, a Native American whose ancestors came from the moon, travels to Manhattan to take revenge for the murder of the tribe elder.

- A young Solomon Barber also likes to gaze up onto "the two Blakelocks in the dining room (a moonlight canvas on the eastern wall and a view of an Indian encampment on the southern)" (p. 246). Later, he turns his attention to the American past, the story of the Native Americans.
- Fogg's contemplation of Blakelock's painting, *Moonlight*, is a key passage of the novel:

  "A perfectly round full moon sat in the middle of the canvas – the precise mathematical center, it seemed to me – and this pale white disc illuminated everything above it and below it: the sky, a lake, a large tree with spidery branches, and the low mountains on the horizon. In the foreground (...) an Indian tepee and a campfire (...) it struck me that Blakelock was painting an American idyll, the world the Indians had inhabited before the white men came to destroy it. (...) the picture had been painted in 1885 (...) almost precisely in the middle of the period between Custer's Last Stand and the massacre at Wounded Knee (...) Perhaps I thought to myself, this picture was meant to stand for everything we had lost. It was not a landscape, it was a memorial, a death song for a vanished world." (pp. 133-135)

Fortune cookie; Moon = symbol of a new beginning
The diversity of the moon motif and its relation to the main character are summarized in the motto Fogg found in his fortune cookie in the Moon Palace restaurant and which he rediscovers in Tesla's autobiography. The moon equally symbolizes a new beginning for Fogg, which is illustrated by him standing on the Californian beach watching the moon rise.

For example:

- The motto in the fortune cookie reads: "The sun is the past, the earth is the present, the moon is the future" (p. 94, 227).

- Fogg has found his place in the world when the moon "had found its place in the darkness" (p. 298). However, Fogg's path has not ended, in the same way that the cycle of the moon never ends.

2) Literature and Philosophy

Apart from the moon motif there are also literary and philosophical themes that occur in *Moon Palace*. This is already implied in the quest for identity which can be found in the interwoven biographies. All three of them (Fogg's, Effing's and Solomon Barber's) are primarily concerned with redrafting their individual identities under specified conditions: Fogg chooses that of the uprooted intellectual; his grandfather, Effing, after his experience of freedom (see p. 142) chooses to go against his father's will and become an artist changing his identity in the desert. Solomon Barber initially feels trapped in his own body but manages to reinvent himself as "the Man Who Wore Hats" (p. 236). Despite their newfound 'freedom', the characters cannot escape their obvious connection to each other. Fogg is forced to reconsider his identity as an "intellectual without background" (see p. 288) and Effing pays off his debt of having denied his son, Solomon, a father by sending him a manuscript of his life story ("Everyone has a right to know about his own past. I can't do much for him but at least I can do that", p. 193).

correlation between name and identity

The topic of the quest for identity contains several motifs, one of which is the repeated importance attached to the meaning of a character's name in relation to his identity. For instance, Solomon's name stands for the connection between the sun and the moon. (see also p. 244)

Uncle Victor tries to invent wild theories about Fogg's name (see p. 6), however, his mother merely chose the name Marco

because she liked it (p. 6) which undermines the theory of name and identity being connected. Effing, however, chooses his name himself which is a biblical pun on the doubting Thomas: „Thus he was Thomas Effing, the man who had fucked his life" (p. 180).
In his youth, Fogg is bullied because of his unusual name, so he also decides to rename himself M.S., which is the abbreviation for manuscript. As his Uncle explains: „Everyone is the author of his own life. (...) The book you are writing is not yet finished. Therefore, it's a manuscript" (p. 7). This metaphor (*life as an invented story*) is in fact an example of the metafictional theme in *Moon Palace*, which continuously returns to the process of writing fictional writing (see chapter 2.3.4). This is also the category where the theatre and play metaphor fits into (seeing *life as a play* and *people as actors*, see p. 204, 207).
The quest for identity also comprises the **search for the cultural identity** which is alluded to in the journeys to the West in search of ancestry as was the case with Uncle Victor:

> *"Now we come to the hard part (...) The endings, the farewells, the famous last words. Pulling up stakes, I think they call it in the Westerns. (...) Who knows if not some new truth will be revealed to me out there?"* (p. 12)

Fogg, on the other hand, attempts to find his cultural identity by studying his environment and himself. For instance, he examines his physical self-destruction: "I was trying to separate myself from my body, taking the long road around my dilemma by pretending that I did not exist" (p.29) and draws the conclusion that "the mind cannot win over matter" (p.29).
Shortly before his mental breakdown, Fogg starts experiencing hallucinations. There are times when he "simply lost track of himself" (p. 29)

Jean-Paul Sartre:
Condemned to liberty

and catches himself chewing 'imaginary food: "Those were the worst moments of all, perhaps, for I realised then that I could no longer trust myself. My mind had gone adrift, and once that happened, I was powerless to stop it" (p.29), which is an example of the **existential concept as analyzed by Jean-Paul Sartre**[12]. In his theory, man's existence is coincidental, non-nonsensical and absurd. Therefore, he has to create his own identity. He is defined through his actions /becomes what he creates. This is what a young Effing experiences under Tesla's humiliating gaze (see p. 142). Fogg's self-observation, that of his surroundings and his temporary feelings of disgust for society, echo Sartre's work, in particular, *Nausea* (1938) where the main protagonist, Antoine Roquentin, a loner living in a provincial town no longer takes life as given. By permanently studying his self, he tries to get to the root cause of his feelings of revulsion for things and people.
Linked to the subject of existence is that of mind and matter. For instance, after the 'Orlando episode', Effing declares that "it's mind over matter, Fogg (...) we've cracked the secret of the universe" (p. 208). In actual fact, he has caught pneumonia. However, as he has chosen his own time of death, his mind has effectively triumphed over matter. This point is also brought up when Uncle Victor and Fogg think up imaginary worlds, when Fogg builds "imaginary furniture from boxes of books" (p. 2) and chews "imaginary food" (p. 29) after losing all his money. The subject of mind and matter is closely interwoven with the subject of realization as implied by Effing's simulated or actual blindness. The reader has to ask himself what is knowledge and how is reality perceived? In Effing's case of 'blindness' Fogg is forced to improve his powers of perception by describing

12 Jean-Paul Sartre (1905-1980) is considered to be the most important philosopher of existentialism as demonstrated in his main work, *Being and Nothingness* (1941).

everything in great detail to Effing. On his way to the Brooklyn museum, Fogg keeps his eyes shut as instructed by Effing and learns how to imagine other people and "what it meant to be blind" (p. 132):

> *"What do you see? And if you see, how do you put it into words? The world enters us through our eyes, but we cannot make sense of it until it descends into our mouths. I began to appreciate how great that distance was: (...) considering how many accidents and losses could occur along the way, it might just as well have been a journey from the earth to the moon."* (p. 118)

Fogg discovers the changeability and uniqueness of things dependent upon their position:

> *"Everything was constantly in flux, and though two bricks in a wall might strongly resemble each other, they could never be construed as identical. More to the point, the same brick was never really the same."* (pp. 118-119)

The permanent changeability of things in the atmosphere, the "hectic motions of molecules, the unceasing explosions of matter, the collisions, the chaos boiling under the surface of all things" (p. 119) and he understands not to take anything for granted.

2.4 Character constellations and characteristics

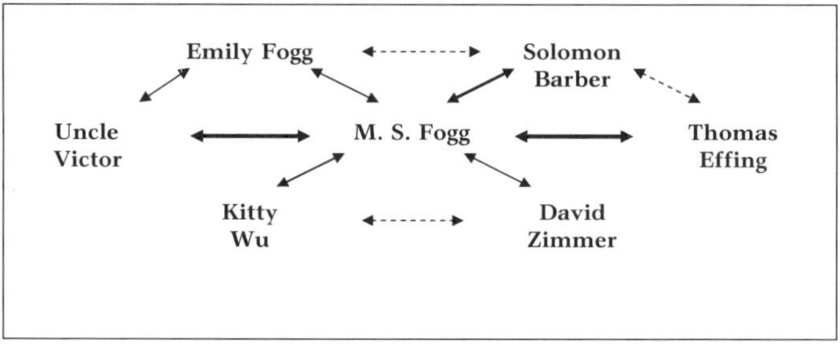

Marco Stanley Fogg

Fogg's character changes throughout the novel (coming-of-age novel). Although Fogg narrates his own life story and judges it, it is an older and more mature Fogg who is judging his younger self (see p. 1, pp. 297/298): Auster: "He [Fogg] is looking back on the way he *used* to think, the way he *used* to interpret the world. It's one of the many follies of his adolescence, a symptom of the madness of those times."[13] Fogg's path can be seen as process of growing up (initiation). He is accompanied by mentors (see Effing, but also Uncle Victor and Solomon Barber).

What he says about his uncle is also true for him: "Like all the Foggs, he had a penchant for aimlessness and reverie, for sudden bolts and lengthy torpors." (p. 5 and see also p. 243). He is a lunatic who experiences the world as full of strange coincidences that are personal to him (see p. 16 or p. 297). Fogg's egocentric approach to life is also demonstrated in his reaction to Barber's confession that he is Fogg's father (see pp. 283).

13 Auster, *The Art of Hunger*, p. 317.

At the beginning of his studies at the age of 18, Fogg tries hard to appear non-conformist, starting with his appearance, as he is always wearing his uncle's old tweed suit: "More than anything else, the suit was the badge of my identity, the emblem of how I wanted others to see me." (p. 15). He stylizes himself as an outsider, as "sublime intellectual" (p. 16). Looking back, Fogg thinks "what a curious figure I must have cut: gaunt, dishevelled, intense, a young man clearly out of step with the rest of the world" (p. 16). Before his uncle's death, he lives the life of a student: he has a part-time job, short flirtations, drinking sprees and "long, utterly silent binges of reading and studying" (p. 17). Following Uncle Victor's death, the death of his last and closest member of his family, his world starts falling apart. Fogg reacts to this in a childish manner – he defiantly shuts himself away from everything.

The narrator stresses that his grief was only one explanation for his life as an outsider. Ultimately, it was the lack of finances, and being too humiliated to confide in anyone about it, which drove him into isolation. However, instead of looking for a job or applying for a grant, Fogg is disgusted by society and decides not to do anything and to wait until his money runs out so he can disappear. In retrospect, he puts this behaviour down to "despair" (p. 20). It is during this time, that Fogg starts reading his uncle's books. He does this to come to terms with his grief, and this demonstrates his emotional side. The contents of the books mould his perception of reality; he starts perceiving it in philosophical and literary terms (see Fogg's lecture on Cyrano and his identification with Raleigh).

During this phase of growing financial struggles, Fogg discovers the advantages of poverty and of a simple life and is surprised that he does not miss life's conveniences. He does not realise that he is slipping into a delusional state (see p. 20). Bit by bit,

he sells off his belongings to be able to cater for his basic needs (bed and board). Due to his tendency towards extremes and his problematic perception of reality he starts analyzing his worsening state of mind like a scientist (see p. 20 and p. 24).
The Book and hunger phase is followed by the experience of real life when he 'moves' into Central Park:

> *"I understood that I had already spent too much of my life living through words, and if this time was going to have any meaning for me, I would have to live in it as fully as possible, shunning everything but the here and now, the tangible, the vast sensorium pressing down on my skin."* (p. 62)

Fogg explains his nihilistic behaviour to the Army psychiatrist as "some form or pattern that would help me to penetrate myself (...) to drift along with the flow of the universe." (p. 78) His experience of being saved by his friends makes him more mature: "From total selfishness, I resolved to achieve a state of total selflessness" (p. 71) but takes him from one extreme to the next. At least, he pays off his debt to Zimmer through the translation. He falls in love with Kitty Wu: She is "without question (...) one of the most memorable things that ever happened to me, and in the end I believe I was fundamentally altered by it." (p. 92). Although in relation to his search for his identity, her importance is only marginal. For instance, when he finds out about Kitty's pregnancy, he is only focused on becoming a father and cannot understand why she wants an abortion. They grow apart and finally separate. Following Solomon's death, he makes one last attempt to get her back, but this is only out of desperation.
When Fogg finds out that Solomon Barber is his father, he reacts with blind rage, "a demonic surge of nausea and disgust" (p. 284); he needs time to adjust to knowing about his heritage, which is no longer shrouded in mystery. After discovering that

Effing's cave has become inaccessible, he rids himself of his rage and frustration by marching through the desert until he reaches the Pacific Coast where he can start a new life. The reference to the moon which has "found its place in the darkness" (p. 298) can be interpreted as Fogg's development coming to an end. He is now finally ready to fit into society.

Uncle Victor

Fogg remembers the "person he loved most in the world" (p. 2) well:

> *"My mother's older brother was a spindly, beak-nosed bachelor of forty-three who earned his living as a clarinetist. Like all the Foggs, he had a penchant for aimlessness and reverie, for sudden bolts and lengthy torpors."* (p. 5)

At the start of the 1950s, even before a young Fogg moves in with him, Victor has to give up his career in the Cleveland Orchestra because of his unreliability. He moves back to Chicago in 1953 and learns to "accept the mediocrity of his career" (p. 5). When his nephew comes to live with him, he supports them by giving clarinet lessons and by playing at family parties with his band, *Moonlight Moods*. One of his character traits is his inconsistency: He is one of those people who "always dreams of doing something else while occupied" (p. 5). He and Fogg share a love of baseball and of *Around the World in 80 Days*: "The hero of that story was named Fogg, of course, and from that day on Uncle Victor called me Phileas as a term of endearment (...)" (p. 6).
Fogg loves his uncle who treated him "less as a child than as a friend, a diminutive and much-adored crony" (p. 6). During their time together, they develop a game thinking up "imaginary worlds that overturned the laws of nature" (p. 6) to escape a reality which they both find hard to bear. Fogg's time with Uncle

Victor, his idol and surrogate family, is a key to his development.

David Zimmer

David Zimmer is Fogg's best friend during their university years. The reader is informed that Zimmer, unlike Fogg, always examines texts thoroughly (see pp. 85/86).

Zimmer reveals his loyalty, cooperation and reliability when he helps Fogg after he has drifted into homelessness. He and Kitty go in search of Fogg and Zimmer takes him in without any questions asked: "He footed the bill for my recovery, and while he never complained about it, I knew his finances were not so solid that he could go on doing it much longer." (p. 84)

Zimmer is originally from New Jersey and starts his course in comparative literature studies at Columbia University at the time of Fogg's recovery. In spite of his talents as a scientist, Zimmer dabbles in poetry. Despite his gratitude, Fogg believes that Zimmer has an ulterior motive in helping him in his recovery: "Now that I had fallen on hard times, perhaps he saw it as an opportunity to gain the upper hand, to right the internal balance of our friendship." (p. 85). Zimmer's girlfriend at the time, a girl "by the name of Anna Bloom or Blume" (p. 86) has just left him and Fogg assumes that his presence might take Zimmer's mind off the pain of rejection.

The narrator does not, however, explain why Fogg and Zimmer lose touch after Fogg moves out. He does not see him again until the spring of 1982 when he runs into him in Manhattan "as chance would have it" (p. 102) and Zimmer has turned into a conventional family man:

> *"We were walking in opposite directions and passed each other by. Then very suddenly, I heard him call out my name. (...) seeing*

Zimmer like that stirred up an entire world of forgotten things for me (...). We stood there on the corner talking about the old days for fifteen or twenty minutes, and then he and his family scampered off to wherever it was they were going." (p. 103)

Fogg finds out that he is now a filmologist and has not written any poems in years. It is this meeting that leads Fogg to consider writing his autobiography (see p. 103).

Kitty Wu

They first meet over the breakfast table in Zimmer's former flat when Fogg turns up and joins them. The other students are quick to notice the affinity between him and Kitty Wu as he happens to be wearing a T-shirt with the logo of Kitty's favourite baseball team, *The New York Mets* (pp. 34-35, "twin sister", p. 34). Kitty Wu is "a Chinese girl of nineteen or twenty with silver bracelets on both wrists and a beaded Navaho band around her head" (p. 35) – the latter is an allusion to the Native American theme. In addition to this, her origins are also important to the novel and its protagonist, Fogg: "Columbus wanted to find an alternative route to China and Marco Polo was the first European to explore China" (see p. 6). In a conspicuous twist, Kitty also seems immediately drawn to Fogg and treats him with a warmth you would normally treat a friend with.
Kitty is modest, emotional and caring; character traits which are illustrated particularly in her concern for Fogg. She and David Zimmer spend weeks looking for Fogg, which at first glance appears to be out of pity (see p. 69) but is actually down to her having fallen in love with him. Unlike Fogg, she is hard-working and eager to earn a living for herself. While studying at Juilliard School, she also has a part-time job at a music and performing art academy in New York.

During Fogg's recovery, she holds back and waits for him to make the first move as she does not want him to think "that she's throwing herself at him" (p. 82). Fogg finds out about Kitty's family background from David Zimmer: Born the daughter of a pre-revolutionary Chinese Kuomintang General and one of his mistresses, she came to America in 1950 and is now orphaned like Fogg. After her birth, her father was appointed Ambassador to Japan, where she grew up. There she was sent to American schools so her English is perfect. Kitty was privy to the luxuries of the upper classes, one of which were her ballet lessons. This is where she developed her love of dancing. She, too, grew up on her own as her half-sister, closest in age, is 10 years older than her. Her mother was very attractive and for that reason was subjected to the petty jealousies of the 64 year-old wife and the 52 year-old first mistress. She died before a 14 year-old Kitty went to boarding school in Massachusetts/USA. Being flexible, down-to-earth, natural, open-minded, hard-working, Kitty quickly settled into her new home country, America. Her inheritance now pays for her studies. At the time of meeting Fogg, she is into her second year at university.

Thomas Effing alias Julia Barber

The character of Fogg's grandfather is as diverse as the identities he assumes throughout the course of his life (first he is Julian Barber, then in the desert he is the hermit Tom, and at the end he adopts Thomas Effing's identity), and just as non-transparent and conflicting. Fogg's time at Thomas Effing's is the key to his development. However, he only finds out about his family connection to the eccentric after Effing's death. The way in which they meet is mysterious: Is it just chance that, of all people, it is Effing's grandson who sees the advert on the notice board and that he is the only one to apply? What role does Effing, who

does not believe in chance but that "[a] force of will that can bend the physical world into any shape I want" (p. 101) and alleges "the hidden purpose of everything" (see p. 101) play? Does Effing know that Fogg is his grandson and is that why he tells him about Solomon Barber? (In his last couple of days, he treats him "as if I were his own flesh and blood" (p. 211). The only thing that is certain is that it is Effing, or rather through Effing's work that Fogg finds out about his family background.
As Fogg is soon to discover, Effing's character is

> *"based on falsehood and deception, it was nearly impossible to know when he was telling the truth. He loved to trick the world with his sudden experiments and inspirations, and of all the stunts he pulled, the one he liked best was playing dead"* (p. 98).

This remark is a double entendre as Fogg not only alludes here to the critically ill wheelchair bound man, but also to the supposedly dead Julian Barber. During their first meeting, they touch on the subject of identity when Fogg has to defend his name (see p. 98). Effing's vision is picked up as a central theme right from the start. When Effing asks him about his eye patches (see p.98). Fogg is open-minded and thinks "there are any numbers of possible answers" (p. 99). Up to the end, Effing's blindness remains a mystery as he stage-manages it by alternating eye patches, dark sunglasses and a blindfold. Sometimes he even leaves his eyes uncovered:

> *"It was hard for me to tell if those eyes could see or not. There were moments when I was convinced that it was all a bluff and that he could see as sharply as I did; at other moments, I became as convinced that he was totally blind. That was how Effing wanted it, of course. He would cast out ambiguous signals (...). It was impossible for me to know what these various costumes meant."* (p. 106)

Effing only comments on his blindness once when he first meets Fogg. Effing alleges that he caused the black-out in New York in 1965 because he had lost his sight shortly before and wished that the entire world would be plunged into darkness. However, he does not explain how he was blinded (see p. 101). Effing's blindness - provided it is not actually faked - is a personal tragedy considering that he had been a painter in his former life as Julian Barber: "the force of light when it hits the eye" (p. 145). The latter may explain his blindness: He may have gazed into the sun for too long or metaphorically, he may have seen the light. In any case, one of Fogg's main duties is to describe the colours, spaces and light to Effing.
From the beginning Fogg points out that he never quite managed to interpret Effing's moods:

> *"The things he said to me, the books he chose for me to read, the strange errands he sent me on – were these parts of an elaborate and obscure plan, or did it only come to look that way in retrospect?"* (p. 105)

Fogg sees Effing as "self-appointed mentor to my inner progress" and "spiritual guide" (p.105). However, at other times, he strikes him as "nothing more than a vicious old man, a burnt-out maniac living in the borderland between madness and earth." (p. 105)
Effing remains an unpredictable character until the end, keeping Mrs. Hume as well as Fogg on their toes whereby Fogg remains uncertain if this is his true identity (see p. 112).

Solomon Barber
According to the first person narrator, the reader expects Fogg to recognise his father at their first meeting, considering that the titles of Solomon Barber's books already indicate a spiritual relationship between the three main characters, Fogg, Effing

and Barber, and they share key themes (*Bishop Berkeley and the Indians, 1947; The lost colonists of Roanoke, 1955; The American Wilderness (1963)*, p. 188).
During their first meeting, Fogg finds out about Solomon Barber's life story and his connection to his mother, Emily. However, Barber omits to tell him that he is his father because he does not want to frighten him off and he also fears that Fogg might reject him on account of his monstrous appearance. Following the scandal over his affair with Emily, Solomon Barber feels upset but not surprised that Emily left him as he had always been aware of his unattractive appearance: "He shrank from mirrors and spent as much time alone as he could. (...) he was an ambulatory freak show, the balloon boy who waddled through gauntlets of laughter and stopped people dead in their tracks." (p. 233)
This has led him to bury himself in books from an early age. He dealt with the absence of his father by writing a fictional novel about it at the age of 17: "(...) trapped in the throes of adolescent tumult, he began to fancy himself an artist, a future genius who would save his soul by pouring his anguish onto paper" (p. 246). He later sends Fogg a copy to "give [him] an idea of the extent to which his father's absence had affected his imagination" (p. 247). This explains Barber's interest in exploring the American West as he wants to gain an understanding of his roots and identity. He finds out about the circumstances surrounding his birth in 1939 from his only surviving relative, Aunt Clara, who lives in the house in Shoreham/Long Island. She explains that his mother rejected him and that it was only his size that had saved him (see pp. 263).
Fogg is the first person to hear about Solomon's life story, as was the case with Effing, and it is Fogg who joins the fragmented pieces together. Barber's affection is shown when he tries to reconcile Fogg and Kitty Wu (see p. 276).

2.5 Annotations

Chapter 1

It was the summer that men first walked on the moon, p. 1: The first moon landing took place in the summer of 1969 with Neil Armstrong, Edwin Aldrin and Michael Collins.
I walked across the desert from Utah to California, p. 1: Reference to the American East-West-Movement during the period of colonization.
Ellis Island, p. 3: Island in New York harbor on which stood an immigration center from 1892-1954 through which all (third-class) immigrants (around 20 million) had to pass.
***Around the World in 80 days*, p. 6**: 1956 film adaptation of Jules Verne's novel with David Niven and Shirley MacLaine about an eccentric Englishman named Phileas Fogg who in 1879 bets that he can travel around the world in 80 days.
Marco Polo, p. 6: Venetian world explorer (1254-1324) who was one of the first Europeans to explore large parts of Asia and China.
Stanley, p. 6: Sir Henry Morton Stanley (1841-1904), British journalist and Africa explorer who found the missing Dr. Livingstone at the Tanganyika Lake.
Cyrano, p. 7: Cyrano de Bergerac (1619-1655), French writer who in 1649 wrote about a fictional journey to the moon.
Little League, p. 7: Baseball League for children.
Swiftian, p. 11: Jonathan Swift (1667-1745), English writer and satirist, he wrote *Gulliver's Travels*.
Schopenhauer, p. 11: Arthur Schopenhauer (1788-1860), German philosopher. The world as will and representation - he justifies the pessimistic doctrine that behind a world of apparition is an aimless irrational and blind will.

Columbus' discovery of America, p. 12: Christopher Columbus (1451-1506) discovered America in 1492 whilst trying to find a new route to India and China.
Malevole, p. 15: Character from Shakespeare's *Twelfth Night, or What you Will.*

Chapter Two

Lazarillo de Tormes, p. 59: a Spanish novel, published anonymously in 1554, and considered to be the first European picaresque novel.
Chappaquiddick, p. 60: Alludes to the scandal surrounding the American Democrat, Edward Kennedy, John F. Kennedy's brother. On 18th July 1969, Edward Kennedy lost control of his car on an excursion to the Island of Chappaquiddick and drove off a bridge into the river. He was unhurt but his 29 year old secretary and presumed lover, Mary Jo Kopechne, drowned. Kennedy was charged with manslaughter and given a two month suspended sentence. This incident marked the end of the Kennedy's hope to regain their leading role in America.
The Chicago Eight, p. 60: Initially seven, then eight demonstrators who had been accused of plotting to riot during the Democrat's party rally in Chicago in 1968. During the trial which lasted for months, several members and representatives of the American left-wing and Anti-culture were called as witnesses, amongst them the writer, Norman Mailer, and the 'LSD-Pope', Timothy Leary.
The Black Panther trial, p. 60: The Black Panther group was founded in 1966 and was a controversial radical Afro-American movement, whose main agenda was to defend the rights of Black. The mention is probably a reference to the trial of the party leader, Bobby Seale who was accused of plotting with the

Anti-War campaigners at the Democratic party conference in 1968.

Another moon landing, p. 61: The Appollo programme saw six moon landings in total. The second took place in November 1969.

Pocahontas, p. 69: (ca. 1595-1617) The daughter of the Indian Chief, Powhatan-Sachem, she is a legendary arbitrator of the English colonialists and the tribes of the Algonkin confederation.

Chapter Three

Kuomintang, p. 82: The Kuomintang is a Chinese political party. They came to power in 1927 on the Chinese Main Land but having lost the Civil War in 1947 against the Communists had to retreat to Taiwan where they continued to rule until 1990.

Lykophrons, p. 85: Greek philosopher and poet (ca. 290 BC).

Giordano Brunos, p. 85: Italian poet and philosopher (1548-1600), who postulated the theory of the infinity and eternity of the universe.

Joseph Joubert, p. 85: French moralist and Essayist (1754-1824).

Mandarin, p. 93: Mandarin (Chinese).

Trotzki, Mao, and the theory of permanent revolution, p. 93: Lew Dawidowitsch Trotzki (1879-1940), a Marxist revolutionary and Soviet politician. He, like Karl Marx, Friedrich Engels and W.I. Lenin, ranks as one of the authorities on socialism. He developed his theory on the working class' permanent revolution up to world revolution. Mao Tse-tung (1893-1976) was the co-founder of the Republic of China. As party leader of China's Communist Party he ruled China dictatorially for nearly 30 years. Trotzki and Mao were symbolic figures in the 1960s' student and anti-war movement.

Chapter Four

Thomas Cole, p. 104: American landscape painter (1801-1848).
Pascal Pensees, p. 104: *Pensées sur la religion et autres sujets* is the work of the French mathematician and philosopher, Blaise Pascale (1623-1662). It was published posthumously in 1670 and is one of the most read philosophical or rather theological texts in European intellectual history.
St Brendan, p. 107: Brendan, the Traveler (ca. 484-577) became famous due to his Navigatio Sancti Brendani, a report about a sea voyage which Brendan is supposed to have undertaken with 12 companions between 565 and 573. The destination was a promising island to the West. In the 19th century it was speculated that this island may have been America. If this is true, Brendan would have discovered it long before Columbus.
Sir John de Mandeville, p. 107: Supposedly the name of the author who wrote about his journey to the Holy Land and the Far East and China in French between 1357 and 1371.
Cabeza de Vaca, p. 107: Spanish sailor and explorer who survived a failed mission for years with the help of Indians who considered him to be a powerful medicine man. He travelled from Florida to California.
Thomas Harriot, p. 107: see chapter 2.3.5.
Ralph Albert Blakelock, p. 129: see chapter 2.3.4 .
Massacre at Wounded Knee, p. 135: see chapter 1.2.
Thomas Moran, p. 137: American painter (1837-1926) who took part in the Hayden expedition in 1871-1872 in the area which is known today as Yellowstone National Park. Moran was the first to paint that particular landscape.
Tesla, p. 138: Nikola Tesla (1856-1943) was a Serbian inventor and electrical engineer. He was the American Thomas Alva Edison's (1847-1931) rival. His most poignant discovery was his contribution to the conventional use of alternating current.

Anasazi, p. 153: Anasazi is the Navajo's word for 'The Elders'. The Anasazi are part of the Pueblo Indians: They lived in caves and in multi-storey clay constructions. Their habitat stretched from Utah and Colorado up to South Mexico. Around 1300 many Anasazi left their towns, the reasons, for which however, remain unknown.

Chapter Five

Hiroshima, p. 218: Port town in the south west of the Japanese island of Honshu. The town became famous after a nuclear bomb was dropped onto it on 6th August 1945 with devastating consequences. The bomb was called 'little boy' (not: Big Boy) and was 'delivered' by the pilot, Paul Tibbets.

Chapter Six

Montaigne, p. 226: Michel de Montaigne (1533-1592), French philosopher, humanist, sceptic, whose work called *Essais* (1580-1588) established the art form of the essay.
(Wall Street) Crash from 1929, p. 246: The stock market crash which started on 24th October with *Black Thursday* and which triggered the world economic crisis.
Navajos, p. 248: North-American Indian tribe.

Chapter Seven

Don Quixote, p. 282: Novel by the Spanish author, Miguel de Cervantes' (1547-1616), *El ingenioso hidalgo Don Quijote de la Mancha* (1605), describes the adventures of a small noble man who has read too many romantic novels, goes mad and henceforth considers himself to be a knight.
Tom Jones, p. 282: Novel by the English author, Henry Fielding (1707-1754). *The History of Tom Jones, a Foundling* describes

the hero, Tom Jones, whilst simultaneously depicting English country life.
Mesa Verde, p. 294: National Park in the south west of Colorado. The park contains over 4000 sites, most importantly, the Anasazi tribal rock dwellings which were only completely explored at the end of the 19th century.
Lake Elsinore, p. 297: Town in Riverside County in California.
Laguna Beach, p. 297: Town South-East of Los Angeles in South California[14].

Translation aids for interpreting *Moon Palace* (English-German)

Theme/Purpose	Thema/Absicht
In his post-modernist novel *Moon Palace,* Paul Auster describes Marco Stanley Fogg's journey of initiation.	In seinem postmodernen Roman Mond über Manhattan behandelt Paul Auster Marco Stanley Foggs Reise zur Ich-Findung.
The author's main concern is the narrator's quest for identity which can be interpreted as a metaphor for life.	Das Hauptinteresse des Autors gilt der Suche nach Identität, die als eine Metapher für das Leben interpretiert werden kann.
The American East-West-Movement- the myth of the Golden West- which is constantly alluded to in the novel - is also seen in this context.	In diesem Kontext steht auch die amerikanische Ost-West- Bewegung- der Mythos vom Goldenen Westen-, auf den im Roman immer wieder angespielt wird.

14 For further annotations see Weishaar, Harald: Paul Auster, *Moon Palace, Annotations and Study Aids*. Stuttgart: Klett, 2005.

Form/Structure	Form/Aufbau
The novel is subdivided into seven chapters which contain a main plot and several subplots.	Der Roman ist in sieben Kapitel unterteilt, die Haupthandlung und mehrere Nebenhandlungen beinhalten.
The three biographies of Fogg, Effing and Barber are interwoven in a very complex way.	Die drei Lebensgeschichten von Fogg, Effing und Barber sind auf eine sehr komplexe Weise ineinander verwoben.
The novel is set in a wide range of places in New York and in the West of the United States.	Der Roman spielt an einer Vielzahl von Orten in New York und im Westen der USA.
Only gradually does the narrative bring to light the fact that Fogg, Effing and Barber are related to each other.	Nur nach und nach enthüllt die Erzählung, dass Fogg, Effing und Barber miteinander verwandt sind.
Using retrospect, the first person narrator and protagonist of the novel describes how he discovered his true identity by chance.	Mit der Verwendung der Retrospektive schildert der Ich-Erzähler und Protagonist, wie er zufällig seine Identität gefunden hat.
The leitmotif of the moon is central to the structure of the novel, though it has a lot of different meanings which cannot be determined completely.	Das Leitmotiv des Mondes hat trotz seiner Bedeutungsvielfalt und Unbestimmbarkeit eine zentrale Bedeutung für den Roman.
The novel starts with a flashback to the year of the first moon landing.	Der Roman beginnt mit einem Rückblick auf das Jahr der ersten Mondlandung.

It ends with Fogg standing on Laguna Beach in California, after a three month march, and watching the moon rise over the Pacific. Thus, the motif of the moon provides the framework for the complex structure of the novel.

Am Ende steht Fogg nach seinem dreimonatigen Marsch am Strand in Laguna Beach/Kalifornien und beobachtet den Mondaufgang. Auf diese Weise umrahmt das Mondmotiv die komplexe Struktur des Romans.

Postmodernist narrative techniques used in *Moon Palace* are fragmentation, cyclical narration, metafiction (stories within the story) and intertextual references.

Postmoderne Erzähltechniken in Moon Palace sind Fragmentarisierung, zyklische Erzählweise, Metafiktion (Geschichten in der Geschichte) und Intertextualität.

Characters

Fogg finds employment as the companion of Thomas Effing, a rich and eccentric old man in a wheelchair. In the end, he discovers that he is his own grandfather.

Charaktere

Fogg findet Anstellung bei Thomas Effing, einem reichen und exzentrischen alten Mann im Rollstuhl. Er findet schließlich heraus, dass dieser sein eigener Großvater ist.

After his breakdown, Fogg finds refuge in Central Park where he suffers badly from flu. It is Kitty Wu, a Chinese ballet dancer, who saves Fogg at the last minute.

Nach seinem Zusammenbruch findet Fogg Zuflucht im Central Park, wo er sich eine schwere Grippe einfängt. Es ist Kitty Wu, eine chinesische Balletttänzerin, die Fogg in der letzten Minute das Leben rettet.

Solomon Barber is a colossal but very intelligent historian who works at a small college in the Midwest.

Solomon Barber ist ein kolossartiger geistreicher Historiker, der an einem kleinen College im Mittleren Westen arbeitet.

After Barber and Fogg's mother, Emily Fogg, had been caught in the act, Emily took the decision to leave Barber and the professor was dismissed.	Als Barber und Foggs Mutter in flagranti erwischt worden waren, beschloss Emily, Barber zu verlassen, und der Professor wurde entlassen.
Style/Language	**Stil und Sprache**
In *Moon Palace* language and style are used to convey the point of view of the narrator.	In Moon Palace werden Sprache und Stil eingesetzt, um die Perspektive des Erzählers zu vermitteln.
The narration is characterized by a mood of reflection which is determined by the perception of events by the first person narrator.	Die Erzählung charakterisiert eine reflektierende Haltung, die sich aus der Ich-Perspektive des Erzählers ergibt.
There is a creative and rich choice of vocabulary which supports the impression that Fogg is a highly educated young man. This is also expressed by the use of metaphorical language.	Es findet sich ein reicher und kreativer Wortschatz, der den Eindruck vermittelt, dass Fogg ein hoch gebildeter junger Mann ist. Dies spiegelt sich auch in dem metaphorischen Sprachgebrauch wider.

2.6 Styles and narrative

Moon Palace contains several narrative styles. They reflect the perceptions and diverse emotions of the first person narrator or imitate his memories, as demonstrated in Fogg's description of the army physical examination:

> *"I distinctly remember sitting on the bench, but after that I see myself lying on the table in another room.* (Jump to the present tense as a stylistic imitation of the envisioned memory) *(...) I don't think I fainted, (...)* (narrator's report) *There was more, there must have been a lot more, but I can't pin down much of it. They gave us lunch somewhere (in the building? In a restaurant outside the building?), but the only thing I remember about the meal is that no one wanted to sit next to me* (rhetorical questions, soliloquy)*" (pp. 75-76).*

In this particular episode, the change of tenses, especially in passages containing flashbacks, is characteristic of a reflective narrative. This ties in with the quest for identity.

> *"Thinking back on it now, I realise how important she was to keeping a measure of stability in the household."* (p. 110)
> *"It almost makes me blush to remember the ridiculous poses I struck back then. I was a grotesque amalgam of timidity and arrogance, alternating between long, awkward silences and blazing fits of rambunctiousness."* (pp. 15)

The narrator's broad education is demonstrated in his use of creative and refined vocabulary, as he constantly refers to terms of literature, art, philosophy and makes use of metaphors:

> *"My origins were a mystery, and I would never know where I had come from. This was what defined me, and by now I was used to*

my own darkness, clinging to it as a source of knowledge and self-respect, trusting in it as an ontological necessity." (p. 286)

This is also shown in the passage where he is agitated about the impending death of his newly-found father:

"I actually felt tears forming in my eyes, and it was only then, sitting in that diner and wrestling with my disappointment, that I understood how fragile my world had become. The egg was slipping through my fingers, and sooner or later it was bound to drop." (p. 289)

In the following passage metaphors are used to accentuate the cyclical structure, and 'the dropping of the last egg' serves to emphasize Fogg's mental breakdown:

"The two eggs I was about to place in a pot of water and boil up for my daily meal slipped through my fingers and broke on the floor. (...) I could not help feeling that this was the cruelest, most terrible thing that had ever happened to me. The eggs landed with an ugly splat. I remember standing there in horror as they oozed out over the floor. (...) I felt as though a star were exploding, as though a great sun had just died. (...) It was all too much for me -the last, imponderable straw. When this happened, I actually sat down and cried." (pp. 41-42)

In this passage, notice that the egg is compared to a big sun, which on a figurative level already points to the loss of the father, as Solomon Barber's nickname is 'Sol' (lat. for sun). However, the egg does not stand for just one thing. There are several other symbolic meanings linked to the egg which also need to be given consideration. Firstly, it is the symbol of fertility, secondly, it is a symbol of perfection and then, in a wider sense, it is thirdly the symbol of the coming together of all creative powers.

In *Moon Palace* styles and narratives are also used to emphasize central topics, for example that of family relations. For instance, Fogg's tirade during a fit of rage ("Say something, you big bag of guts, say something or I'll smash you in the mouth", p. 284) is reminiscent of his grandfather's obscene use of language ("Ignorant asshole. Fuck Edison", p. 127).

2.7 Approaches to *Moon Palace*

1) The moon as a motif and the end of the novel

In an interview with Larry McCaffery and Sinda Gregory from 1992, Paul Auster explains the central motif - the moon - and the novel itself as a **criticism of the American idea of progress**. The author explains that the end of the novel can be interpreted as Fogg being ready to start his life (as an adult):

> *"The moon is many things all at once, a touchstone. It's the moon as myth, as 'radiant Diana, image of all that is dark within us'; the imagination, love, madness. At the same time, it's the moon as object, as celestial body, as lifeless stone hovering in the sky. But it's also the longing for what is not, the unattainable, the human desire for transcendence. And yet it's history as well, particularly American history. First, there's Columbus, then there was the discovery of the West, then finally there is outer space: the moon as the last frontier. But Columbus had no idea that he'd discovered America. He thought he had sailed to India, to China. In some sense, Moon Palace is the embodiment of that misconception, an attempt to think of America as China. But the moon is also repetition, the cyclical nature of human experience. There are three stories in the book, after all, and each one is finally the same. Each generation repeats the mistakes of the previous generation. So it's also a critique of the notion of progress. And if America is the land of progress, what are we to make of ourselves then? And so on and so on and so on. Fogg wends his way among all those ideas, this pinball machine of associations, struggling to find a place for himself. By the end of the book I think he manages to get somewhere. But he only reaches the beginning, the brink of his adult life. And that's where we leave him – getting ready to begin"*[15].

15 Auster, *The Art of Hunger*, p. 317.

2) *Moon Palace* as a picaresque novel

Werner Reinhart interprets *Moon Palace* as a contemporary picaresque novel. He begins by listing **four theses for the reactivation of the picaresque novel in a Reaganist America**. Ronald Reagan's presidency (1981-1989) was dominated domestically by economic optimism (tax cuts) and externally by anti-Communism. Reagan's government invested heavily in the build-up of arms (national debt), cooperated with every anti-Communist Third World regime and secretly participated in wars, such as that against the Nicaraguan government.
Reinhart's theses are as follows:

1. The domestic and socio-political shortcomings of the Reagan era triggered an offensive politicization of the American novel culture.
2. One indication of the politicization is the renaissance of the picaresque narratives, tales and world interpretation patterns.
3. The picaresque narrative was reinvented as a form of political narrative in the 1980s in America.
4. The debate Reagan's America sparked triggered a dedicated literary expression of oppositional ideologies and norms and values[16].

Reinhart then goes on to cite the characteristics of the picaresque novel as they appear in *Moon Palace:*

1. The character in a picaresque novel is almost always - at least from the time he/she becomes an orphan - a (social) outsider.
2. He/she is defined by his/her desire to belong and to seek emotional compensation. As orphaned (orphaned, semi-orphaned or the refusal of any parental contact) individuals, they are

16 Reinhart, Werner: *‚Fiction as strange as the world I live in'*: Paul Austers *Moon Palace* als zeitgenössische Pikareske. http://www.oberschulamt-freiburg.de/gym/faecher/english/eng_jae/auster/_start.htm (August 2006)

unable to form long-lasting relationships and try to compensate for the absence of their parents by trying to substitute them. The quest for the mother or father is fundamental as a motif in a picaresque novel.

3. The picaresque world is governed by the law of fate and unpredictability[17].

3) History in *Moon Palace*

In the book, *The World that is the Book*, **Aliki Varvogli** examines the **subjective and objective experience of historical events** in *Moon Palace:*

> *"The question of the distinction between subjective and objective experience lies at the heart of this book. Most of the historical facts mentioned in the narrative are in some way connected with the experience of the protagonist. History is experienced subjectively, made to mirror inner states and anxieties. It is non-linear, made-up of arbitrary connections which only acquire meaning for the person who makes them. For Fogg, the neon sign of the Chinese restaurant Moon Palace, which he sees from his window, serves as unifying symbol, bringing the universal into the personal (...) The fundamental truth that Fogg seeks is not a universal truth, the truth of historical fact. The only accessible truth, which is the truth of art, is to be arrived by finding one's own place in the world and its events (...)* Moon Palace *is a quest for self-knowledge, but it is also a quest to decipher the American landscape and to understand the land's history."*[18]

17 Ibid.

18 Varvogli, *The World that is the Book: Paul Auster's Fiction* (Liverpool, Liverpool University Press, 2001), pp. 130.

3. Topics and assignments

***Moon Palace* and Postmodernism**	**Hint**
▶ Place the novel *Moon Palace* into the correct literary context of post-modernism and debate the author's intentions.	see chapter 2.1
▶ Discuss the form and function of the novel's narrative structure.	see chapter 2.3
▶ Study individual chapters and assess their importance for Fogg's quest for identity.	see chapter 2.3
▶ Analyze the moon motif and the role of fate.	see chapter 2.3, 2.7
▶ Which linguistic and stylistic characteristics define *Moon Palace*, and what is their function?	see chapter 2.6
▶ Analyze the story of *Moon Palace* using the interpretation aids available.	see chapter 2.7

2) Topic: New York and the American West – History and Myth in *Moon Palace*	**Hint**
▶ What picture does the author paint of New York and the myth of the American West? Discuss.	see chapter 1.2, 2.3, 2.7
▶ Examine the importance of the journeys to the west for the main character's quest for identity.	see chapter 2.3, 2.4
▶ Examine the principle relationships in *Moon Palace*.	see chapter 2.4

▶ Analyze the autobiographical elements in *Moon Palace*.	see chapter 1.1, 2.7
▶ Set *Moon Palace* into the correct historical context and assess the accuracy of the historical events portrayed.	see chapter 1.2, 2.5,2.7

3) Topic: Further studies of *Moon Palace*	Hint
▶ Interpret *Moon Palace* using external sources, such as Raleigh's poems.	see chapter 2.5, 5
▶ Analyse Fogg's character using the passage on Fogg's conversation with the military psychiatrist.	
▶ Discuss the role of art in *Moon Palace*.	
▶ Write a review of *Moon Palace*.	

4. The Critics

Auster's work has not been as well received in America as it has been in Europe due to American critics traditionally being tied to more conventional, critical views[19]. The author took the initially negative reception in the press rather with humour:

> *"People can say whatever they want; they're entitled to misread books in any way they choose. It takes time for the dust to settle, and every writer has to be prepared to listen to a lot of stupidities when his work is discussed. The reviewing situation is particularly bad here after all. (...) we probably have the lowest standard of literary journalism anywhere. Some of the people who review books strike me as quasi-illiterate (...) theirs are the opinions that circulate, at least at the beginning of a book's life."*[20]

Paul Auster is mainly successful in Europe:

Success in Europe

> *"He has also often been described as European, an adjective – used in praise on this side of the Atlantic, occasionally in bafflement on his own – which apparently sums up the coolly detached tone and the occasional eerie hint of existentialism behind his pacy plots. Auster's work has always been more popular in Europe than in the US. In 1996 Jack Lang, France's former culture minister, claimed that Auster was the only 'great young writer' in America. Salman Rushdie, a close friend, says Auster has 'a European sensibility brought to bear on entirely American subject matter (...)"*[21]

19 Translation of *Einschätzungen von Ann Lauterbach und Craig Raine* in Hadley Freeman: American Dreams. http://www.guardian.co.uk/books/2002/oct/26/fiction.fashion#article_continue.

20 Auster, *The Art of Hunger*, pp. 303.

21 Hadley Freeman: American Dreams. In: The Guardian, 26.10.2002. Der Artikel ist im Internet zu finden, unter http://books.guardian.co.uk/departments/generalfiction/story/0,6000,819191,00.html#article_continue. [February 2009].

James Bone offers a positive view of the often criticized chance-motif in *Moon Palace*. According to him, it symbolizes Auster's existentialist attitude:

> *"Auster's plots are sometimes criticised for their contrived use of chance, which leaves the reader wanting for 'the suspension of disbelief'. Characters' lives lurch from one coincidence to another. But chance – and its ultimate corollary, mortality - is Auster's grand existentialist theme."*[22]

It should be noted that *Moon Palace* was appraised as well as criticized for its link between traditional and post-modern narratives. Another critic, Paul Ingendaay, voices an ambivalent opinion in the FAZ newspaper (on 22.09.1990): *'Although the novel is an interesting story, part Bildungsroman, part western and road movie, but so much happens in it that it reminds me of a construction kit of American urban myths and technical genre embellishments.'*[23]

22 James Bone: Dem old Bush Blues. In: The Times, Weekend Review, 17.4.2004, http://www.timesonline.co.uk/article/0,,592-1075597_2,00.html

23 Ingendaay, Paul: *Wenn alles ins Wanken gerät. Die Magie der Wörter und der Mond über Manhattan.* In: Frankfurter Allgemeine Zeitung, 22. September 1990.

5. Further Material

1) Sir Walter Raleigh's lyrics

Before his breakdown, Fogg is fascinated by and identifies himself with the Elizabethan lyrics of Sir Walter Raleigh (1554-1618) which were written prior to the poet's execution (see p. 42). Auster even wrote an essay about Raleigh's death (*The Death of Sir Walter Raleigh*, in *The Art of Hunger*, pp. 75-82). Raleigh's popular poems - see for example Abrams, M. H. (Hrsg.): The Norton Anthology of English Literature. Third Ed., Bd 1, New York: W. W. Norton, 1974, p. 755 & p. 750 or http://www.poemhunter.com/sir-walter-raleigh/poet-7013/[24] - can be used to compare the conception of the main protagonist as well as for the intertextual references of *Moon Palace*.

2) Auster's reflections on the chance-motif

While Fogg's mentor, Effing, disputes the existence of chance, Fogg believes and surrenders to it, for instance when, having lost all his money, he moves to Central Park. For Paul Auster, chance is important, too, as he emphasizes in an interview with Larry McCaffery and Sinda Gregory:

'I see myself as realist in the strictest meaning of that word. Chance is part of that reality: Chance events form our entire life, the unknown overwhelms us in a sheer regularity. Despite this, it is generally believed that you can go over the top with fantasy in a novel. Everything which does not seem plausible has to therefore be constrained, factitious and unreal. I can't imagine what kind of reality these people live in but it's certainly not mine. It's paradox to say it but maybe they have spent too much time reading. The conventions of the so-called realistic literature have penetrated their minds to the extent

---

24

that they can't understand reality properly anymore (...) Things can happen from one minute to the next. Our live-long certainties about this life can change in the space of a second. To clarify it i philosophical terms: I'm talking about the power of Chance. Our live does not belong to us, it belongs to the world; we can try to make an effort to understand this as much as we like but our mind simply transcends us. We encounter the inexplicable everywhere we go. The consequences can be very frightening – but also very comical'.[25]

25 Translated from Auster, *Die Kunst des Hungers*, pp. 204-206.

Literature

Primary Literature

Auster, Paul: *Moon Palace* (Faber and Faber Limited, London, 1990). All page references refer to this edition.

Auster, Paul: *Mond über Manhattan.* Dt v. Werner Schmitz. Reinbek bei Hamburg: Rowolt Taschenbuch Verlag, 2006.

Auster, Paul: *The Art of Hunger. Essays, Prefaces, Interviews and the Red Notebook* (New York, Penguin, 1997).

Auster, Paul: *Die Kunst des Hungers.* Dt. v. Werner Schmitz. Reinbek bei Hamburg: Rowohlt Taschenbuch Verlag, 2000.

Auster, Paul: *Hand to Mouth. A chronicle of early failure* (New York, Picador, 2003).

Auster, Paul: *Von der Hand in den Mund: eine Chronik früher Fehlschläge.* Dt. v. Werner Schmitz. Reinbek bei Hamburg: Rowohlt Taschenbuch Verlag, 1998.

Secondary Literary

Herzogenrath, Bernd: *An Art of Desire: Reading Paul Auster* (Amsterdam, Rodopi, 1999). (Ref. *Moon Palace*, pp. 115-156)

Ingendaay, Paul: *Wenn alles ins Wanken gerät. Die Magie der Wörter und der Mond über Manhattan.* In: Frankfurter Allgemeine Zeitung, 22. September 1990.

Kammerer, Hilmar: *Paul Auster, Moon Palace.* Freising: Stark, 2001.

Klepper, Martin: *Moon Palace (1989): Marcos Mondfahrt.* In: Martin Klepper: Pynchon, Auster, DeLillo: Die amerikanische Postmoderne zwischen Spiel und Rekonstruktion. Frankfurt und New York: Campus Verlag, 1996, pp. 284-298.

Michlin, Monika: *Bitter Sweet Gravity: Moon Palace.* In: *QWERTY, 6* (1996), pp. 217-224.

Putjenter, Britta: Paul Auster, *Moon Palace, Annotations and Study Aids.* Stuttgart, Düsseldorf, Leipzig: Klett, 2001.

Schuhmacher, Karl Eduard: *Lektürehilfen Paul Auster, Moon Palace,* Stuttgart, Düsseldorf, Leipzig: Klett, 7, Auflage 2005.

Springer, Carsten: *A Paul Auster Sourcebook* (Frankfurt am Main, Peter Lang, 2001).

Springer, Carsten: *Crises: The Works of Paul Auster* (Frankfurt am Main, Peter Lang, 2001).

Springer, Carl Carsten: *Paul Auster*. In: Kritisches Lexikon zur fremdsprachigen Gegenwartsliteratur (KlfG), 59. Nlg, 10/2002.

Varvogli, Aliki: *The World that is the Book: Paul Auster's Fiction* (Liverpool, Liverpool University Press, 2001).

Weisenburger, Steven: *Inside Moon Palace*. In: Dennis Barone (Hrsg): Beyond the Red Notebook: Essays on Paul Auster (Philadelphia, University of Pennsylvania Press, 1995), pp. 129-142.